# Deputy Headship

## by
## Peter Lawley

Longman

In association with
The National Association of Head Teachers

Longman Group UK Limited
Longham House, Burnt Mill, Harlow, Essex CM20 2JE

First published 1988

**British Library Cataloguing in Publication Data**

Lawley, Peter
    Deputy headship.
    1. Great Britain. Comprehensive schools.
    Deputy head teachers. Role
    I. Title
    373.11'41

    ISBN 0-582-02362-9

Printed and bound in Great Britain by
Biddles Ltd, Guildford and King's Lynn

# Contents

# Preface and Acknowledgements

I first became interested in the idea of writing a book on Deputy Headship after several years' service as a Deputy Head. Learning the job by trial and, more often, error, I realised that there was no publication in existence which really addressed itself to the challenges, problems and satisfactions I had experienced. The reason the task of writing such a book had apparently defeated previous writers soon became obvious. There was an infinite variety of forms which Deputy Headship could take, to a degree which made generalisation sometimes seem pointless. In addition, given the significance of the subject, relevant research studies and conclusions were somewhat exiguous.

To overcome these obstacles to clarity, it was necessary to hold in balance a number of different theoretical perspectives and beliefs about education, schooling and management. There was a tension to overcome between existing conventional wisdom about the running of schools, and a particular view of things which the Deputy Head encounters in daily experience.

This is a practical book, encompassing questions of administration, record-keeping, regular dealings with pupils, parents and teachers; but also the equally inescapable exigencies of power, status, participation and accountability in management. The former set of functions and relationships must take place within a climate of the latter.

I would not expect every practising Deputy Head to agree with all that I have written, nor necessarily to accept my personal biases and points of emphasis; these are perhaps inevitable when practitioners produce studies of their own field of endeavour.

I must thank the National Association of Head Teachers, the National Union of Teachers and the Secondary Heads' Association for providing copies of documents and dealing with my correspondence, and the various publishers who have given permission for the reproduction of copyright material. To Sheila Butteriss, I must express my sincere gratitude for her patience in deciphering and typing the manuscript.

Peter Lawley

*For Jean*

# 1 School management and the Deputy Head

A few years ago, when asked what a Deputy Head did, most teachers would have been hard-pressed to answer at any length. They might have named one or two tasks such as timetabling or helping with acute crises, but few would have expected the person involved to do more than get on with a variety of rather routine duties.

Developments in school management over the years have at last affirmed the position of Deputy Head. The process of affirmation has been gradual and uneven and is still going on at a time when the job is subject to considerable local variations from school to school. These variations will be acknowledged throughout this book, as different aspects of a Deputy Head's experience and responsibility are explored. To a large extent Deputy Headship is dependent upon the nature of Headship – whether it is exercised as an executive management function, as a set of historically derived role expectations, or as the leadership mission of an inspired individual. The way in which Heads seek to realise their own particular conception of their role is a dominant but not the sole factor in the way Deputy Headship is exercised. This means that any account of Deputy Heads must be informed by an understanding of the nature of Headship as well as of the origins of Deputy Headship. These origins suggest something of the uncertainty, improvisation and even downright rivalry and conflict between Heads and Deputies in the past. Many dilemmas remain as the historical legacy of a dubious job identity manifests itself in contemporary daily experience. Nevertheless, progress is being made towards a more universal rationale for Deputy Headship, which still embraces the diversity of forms it may take.

# Heads and Deputies

In their attempt to define the job of the secondary Head, Morgan, Hall and Mackay (1983) found that the nature of Headship had changed considerably in the twentieth century, 'not so much in the extent and scope of their constitutional powers, but in the style and execution of those powers' (p. 9). This was part of the move, as they saw it, from 'autocrat' to 'chief executive'; the autocratic model having been challenged as early as the 1930s by the intermediate style of 'leading professional' which perhaps only became fully established as an accepted alternative by the 1960s. Even then, the autocratic approach to Headship was still widely practised and continues to be so in spite of changing external pressures upon the school.

The well-known account by Baron (1956) of the 'Headmaster Tradition' helps to explain how autocratic assumptions and expectations linger and remain, despite rhetoric to the contrary. They still have unpredictable effects upon team management, which are examined later in this book. The success of Arnold of Rugby from 1828–42, within the rapid development of public schools in the nineteenth century, lay in establishing the idea of a school as a moral and religious community. He also established a sense of mission as a part of the purpose of Headship, which was shared by other famous figures of the time. This helped to define Headship clearly, while the status and expectations laid upon other teachers remained vague. In consequence, power was bestowed exclusively upon the Head, who in turn held almost total responsibility for the success or failure of the school. Such management structures as existed would be informed and constrained by this general climate. Deputy Heads are not generally referred to in documents of the time, although there is evidence to show that other masters gained *de facto* positions of responsibility and influence the more a particular school expanded.

Nineteenth-century schools had inherited members of staff holding the position of 'Usher' or 'Under Master' which dated back to the Endowed Grammar Schools of the fifteenth century (Burnham, 1968). With security of tenure, and frequent independent responsibility for the running of the lower school, it became common for conflict to occur, 'characterised by personal feuds, clashes of personality and quarrels over teaching methods, choice of text books and appropriation of fees' (*ibid*, p. 170). The scale of the problem grew with the rise of the autocratic Head, so much so that the Clarendon and Taunton Commissions, in 1864 and 1868 respectively, removed the Ushers' rights to security of tenure.

If total chaos had been avoided by these measures, the position of Deputy Head (known as 'First Assistant' in the elementary schools) lacked clarity, apart from the fact that the making of the appointment was to be firmly in the hands of the Head, and the appointee would be the Head's Deputy by virtue of holding the rank second to that of Head. Burnham (*ibid*) describes the range of views held then about what Deputy Heads should contribute as individuals, including having supplementary qualifications to the Head, being a particularly good teacher, and having the ability to deputise in the Head's absence. This range of desirable qualities remains what is often still specified today, without recognition of the different scale of operations required in the management of a large school. An emphasis placed upon the dominant Head perhaps inevitably encouraged the rise of the Head's 'handy person' in competition for preferment through the creation of organisation for its own sake, rather than for clearly thought-out educational reasons. In his novel, *The Longest Journey*, E.M. Forster's character, Mr Pembroke, is just such a person in a second-rate public school early in the twentieth century:

> . . . he organised. If no organisation existed, he would create one. If one did exist, he would modify it. 'An organisation', he would say, 'is not after all an end in itself. It must contribute to a movement'. When one good custom seemed likely to corrupt the school, he was ready with another; he believed that without innumerable customs there was no safety, either for the boys or men. Perhaps he is right and always will be right. Perhaps each of us would go to ruin if for one short hour we acted as we thought fit, and attempted the service of perfect freedom. The school caps, with their elaborate symbolism were his; his the many-tinted bathing-drawers, that showed how far a boy could swim; his the hierarchy of jerseys and blazers. It was he who instituted Bounds, and Call, and the two sorts of exercise-paper, and the three sorts of caning, and 'The Sawstonian', a bi-terminal magazine. His plump finger was in every pie. The dome of his skull, mild but impressive, shone at every masters' meeting. He was generally acknowledged to be the coming man. (Forster, 1960, p. 48).

Pembroke's modern equivalents are still commonly considered to be 'good managers' and suitable Deputy Head material, if only because many a weary Head is pleased to have the services of an administrative factotum to provide relief from mundane tasks and make more time in which to enjoy the exercise of authority. Others see their job as being to sponsor the progress of the Pembrokes of this world as examples to others of what can be achieved by well-motivated individuals. In both cases, this type of Head, though still to be found, is becoming increasingly outmoded as new styles of management and beliefs about the nature of schools take hold. However, for power to be shared, for a senior management team to be built up as a group which shares leadership and involves itself in mobilising the energy and commitment of staff through the school's formal structures and informal processes, considerably enhanced demands on skills and qualities have to be made of Deputy Heads as well as of Heads. These will be explored later in more detail, particularly in Chapters 4 and 5.

## A complementary relationship

The exercise of successful Headship lies partly in avoiding influences which obstruct the sharing of responsibility between all staff for what is happening in the school. These influences may include inheritors of the troublesome Usher tradition when a Deputy is not working well, quite apart from the officiousness of latter-day Pembrokes. They constrain good Headship, which works as a positive, creative force, acting through people's desire to contribute by co-ordinating the efforts and enthusiasm of a group of professionals. It is also sufficiently receptive to ideas and influences in the school, which it encourages in order to remain both open and responsive to changes. These changes may include an alteration in the pupil intake of the school, the emergence of a new group of staff distinguished by qualifications and interest, or opportunities for curriculum innovation.

Effective Headship is greatly enhanced by the presence of effective Deputies. Too often 'effectiveness' relates to administrative efficiency alone, necessary as that is. In this context, it should be taken to mean the ability to understand and share in all discussions and policy formulation involved in managing the school. The concept of leadership which is open to ideas and influences throughout the school can be realised through the work and example of a senior management team. In its own values and procedures it forms a microcosm of the ideal of shared decision-making, and arrival at agreement through a consensus shared by fellow professionals. This is a long way from the model of autocratic Headship in which the Deputy was generally required to act as no more than a go-between for the staffroom and the Head's study.

As Headship and Deputy Headship are seen as being offices exercised in a spirit and expectation of partnership, so the skill and need to recognise individual strengths and weaknesses become important among senior staff. Bringing forward positive attributes and qualities is better than imposing rigid job descriptions on a role arrived at by previous incumbents of the post. For example, a Deputy with known union credentials may be better at negotiation during industrial action than an exasperated Head who is prone to loss of temper. A Deputy who has a special knowledge of youth work and is effective in chairing small groups may be better at leading the staff involved in developing the work of the form tutor than someone whose standing with departmental heads and meticulous attention to detail equips them as an effective timetabler. This allows for a team to be built up on the basis of individual strengths and personalities. The way in which the team works within itself and interacts with the rest of the school will be explored in depth in Chapter 5. Its operations are an important part of the way in which present-day Deputy Headship has developed.

Deputy Headship suffers from the danger of becoming a dumping ground for a succession of roles and functions which it has not proved possible to allocate elsewhere. It is necessary to come to terms with the need to accomplish administrative tasks of the school while at the same time ensuring the Deputy carries out management functions properly. This is still the most uncertain aspect of the position's establishment, when Deputies are sometimes swamped by quantities of petty administrative detail. Uncertainty is further fostered by conflicting expectations from governors, local authority officers and even from staff within the school. For this reason the role of Deputy Head is explored not as a single entity, but in the various forms it can take, at all times keeping sight of the practical requirements of running schools. As Chapter 3 demonstrates, special personal qualities, allied to an ability to gather the technical knowledge relevant to a particular institution, are necessary in order to work well with staff, given the needs of a particular school. Here, the absence of a rigid standardised role specification, intended to be applied nationally, is a positive advantage.

## External influences

If Headship has changed greatly within schools, then it is at the same time being affected by a much increased set of expectations and pressures from outside. Much has resulted from political interest in the curriculum since the 1970s, leading to measures like the hastily imposed General Certificate of Secondary Education examination system. Rapidity of change has led to a situation in which it is necessary to inform and discuss implications with teachers, to build up databanks in the school concerning deployment of staff and alternatives available (such as second teaching subjects), and to support individuals left bewildered by the changes affecting them. Above all, the changed climate in which every member of the public who feels he or she knows something about education tends to comment forcibly upon it, has altered the immediate atmosphere surrounding schools. Local pressure groups, political and non-political, are likely to make their presence felt through the governors and may do so more strongly under the enhanced powers of governors bestowed by the 1986 (No 2) Education Act. The pressures applied here, reinforced by strong local and national media interest in schools, have special implications. Heads, while not seeking to escape their responsibility to be accountable to the communities their schools serve, nevertheless have to take finely balanced decisions about how to present and explain matters affecting the school in the light of the likely reactions and assumptions of others. A frequent example is the misleading reporting of examination results in which schools from socially privileged areas are compared crudely with the less privileged. The method or presentation of data and editorial comment in a local newspaper may do nothing to point out the relative success of the socially deprived school in producing better results than would normally be expected from its intake, as well as achieving success in fields other than those of examination grades. A Head, supported by a good team of Deputies, is able to take advice and consider a course of action and all its implications before proceeding further; for instance by releasing a statement to the paper, by writing to parents, or by declining to react publicly.

Another set of external influences has increased the level of constraint upon Headship while at the same time creating a demand for increased technical knowledge about what may be done and how to respond to problems. These lie in the fields of the legal requirements now placed upon schools in a variety of areas. The application of health and safety at work legislation makes the school premises subject to inspection from outside, and by accredited trade union health and safety representatives. The follow-up of reported faults has legal implications, and decisions sometimes have to be taken on whether or not particular areas of a school or its facilities should be used because of the very specific liability in case of accident.

Employment legislation demands care in the drafting of advertisements, in what is actually said at interviews and in avoiding the use of any language which could be taken as discriminatory. Likewise, children with special educational needs are subject to the provisions of the 1981 Act; and procedures for the exclusion of pupils are subject to the 1986 (No 2) Act. Deputies may have a direct responsibility for implementing such administrative details in school, as well as forming part of a team in which each individual possesses detailed technical knowledge of the relevant legislation and can contribute to discussion on critical cases as they arise.

In addition to these influences, the local authorities themselves have developed corporate management systems. These, more than in the past, may involve the Head in direct contact with local authority engineers, planners and architects, as well as various privately contracted firms, over the maintenance and repair of buildings. At the same time authority-based support in the form of clerks, advisers and welfare staff has tended to diminish due to financial cutbacks, with a resulting increase in administrative work at school level. The extended range of skills required in managing additional physical aspects of a large site, over and above the educational leadership of the institution, present another aspect of the requirements to be met within a successful management team.

The concentration of managerial responsibility on one person places considerable demands upon the office of Head. In a large school these have become essentially unrealistic, despite the historic nature of public expectations. If Heads have to operate in a style more akin to that of an executive in charge of a large workplace, with the added moral and social responsibility required from a leading educator, then a level and quality of support is inevitably required. This has to be found from a small team of Deputy Heads – two or three, who either form or take part in the senior management team. Their skills and training stem from the requirements of Headship, as they relate to its functions so closely. This places the demands to be made of the Deputies on a different level from those of other teachers, including those involved in the middle management, because their responsibilities always have a broad, whole-school nature.

## Changing schools

Looking within schools, it will be found that the variety of external influences for change have been matched by an increasing internal complexity. With comprehensive reorganisation in the 1960s, the size of a typical secondary school more than doubled. Secondary-modern and grammar schools with between 400 and 600 on roll gave way to comprehensives of 1200 pupils upwards. At first, many Heads inherited from the old system made little effort to change their policies, except to continue with their old beliefs on a larger scale. The old sense of loyalty and implicit shared values, it was felt, would win the day. If it did not, scapegoats such as the poor home background of pupils, or the poor training of young teachers in colleges, could always be found.

In schools which realised that change meant their successful operation could not just be left to chance, new structures began to emerge to support identified needs. The desire to provide a high quality diversified curriculum for all pupils, rather than a traditional grammar-school curriculum or its watered-down version, became one important goal. It was quickly appreciated that in large schools it was essential to ensure all pupils should have the opportunity to become known really well by at least one member of staff, and that no individual's particular needs or problems should be overlooked simply because the size of the institution rendered it impersonal. For pastoral care to be effective, it had to be planned for, and its success monitored. This meant that staff had to be appointed, trained and to work within a management structure which would ensure quality through teacher support and motivation. The Deputy Head's specialised management function for pastoral care here is described in Chapter 2.

In the development of the curriculum, as in pastoral care, staff needed the opportunity for systematic training and enhancement of skills. This could be effected through school staff development policies involving courses, the assistance of local authority advisers, and making opportunities for new experiences for staff within the school itself. The development of a nationally imposed grant-related in-service and training system for teachers in 1987 compelled many schools to go through a process of identifying needs in a hurry. A system which takes a Deputy Head several years to implement with the full involvement of staff was enforced in a few weeks!

If management responsibilities of senior staff had grown beyond all recognition in the course of comprehensive reorganisation, then the desire to improve and develop practice, and to seek a rationale for school management, posed a number of questions. Was it possible to train people in management skills? Were these skills the same in schools as in the local factory or supermarket? Were schools different from or the same as industrial concerns in their purpose and values? Was 'management' just a gimmick sought after – either by ambitious individuals to further their careers, or as a mystique to avoid a more basic discussion of the political and moral realities faced by schools in modern society?

These questions continue to be much discussed as management courses have grown – conducted by local authority advisers, Her Majesty's Inspectorate, private organisations and, notably, the Open University, which offers an Advanced Diploma in Educational Management. Such courses have legitimated educational management as a field of study and training, as well as identifying the tasks and needs of teachers at different levels. Most committed heads of department or pastoral heads would expect to attend courses on the management aspects of their work, or to prepare them for new responsibilities.

# The status of Deputy Headship

However, the management in education movement, as manifested in its courses, conferences and literature, has largely omitted the study of Deputy Headship. Headship itself has been the subject of a major study (Morgan, Hall, Mackay, *op.cit.*), and literature on subject-department and pastoral-staff leadership – 'middle management' – is also available in quantity. Perhaps the view of the all-powerful Head continues to dominate the assumptions of writers and researchers at the expense of the study of how teams manage large schools, implying as this does the contribution of high quality Deputy Headship.

One of the most notable exceptions to this state of affairs was to be found in the Open University Course 'Management and the School' (E323, Block 4, 1981) in which an attempt was made to summarise the sparse literature and research on the subject in order to try to define the Deputy Head's role in primary and secondary schools. A brief, historical section refers to the 1956 Burnham Report on teacher salaries which established that all schools above a minimum size should have a post designated 'Deputy Head'. This is followed by a stipulation of the 1978 Burnham Report that in schools of group 7 and 8, a Senior Master or Mistress post could be established, and in group 9 schools or higher, a second Deputy could be appointed at the Authority's discretion. The Senior Master or Mistress was paid at the same level as the Deputies, and actually redesignated 'Deputy Head' in the salary award of 1987. In effect large schools had a senior management team which generally included three Deputy Heads.

The section continues by examining the tendency for the definition of the Deputy's role to suffer from vagueness: this is thought to be largely the responsibility of Heads for leaving the role in a state of ambiguity. Delegation of authority, which has become essential given the size of schools, helps to define the role of the Deputy in any specific place, but post-holders were often in a position of having to administer policies which they had not been involved in at their formative stages. The position of having to undertake responsibility without power was found to be a common complaint, although more recent evidence suggested that membership of a school management team allowed for fuller participation in school policy formulation.

It is apparent here that no single style of Headship had been discerned; rather a number of approaches are outlined, varying from the partnership of team management to a continuation of the old dominance by one person of an essentially authoritarian structure. The single most influential factor in defining the Deputy's role lay in the expectations of an individual Head, although the role expectations of other staff had their effect.

The course text suggests two further way of examining the Deputy Head's role: by looking at the place it occupies within the management structure, and by accounting for the activities performed in the post. Structure was again related to the size of school, and the increase in the number of Deputies allowed for a degree of specialisation. This is explored further in Chapter 2, as is the range of activities Deputies are called upon to·perform.

In attempting to arrive at a model of Deputy Headship, it is suggested that:

> The power and authority associated with Headship must be shared with the Deputies. . . . The willingness of the Head to delegate real authority to Deputies depends in part on good relations among these senior managers and on the basis of shared values. Where the Deputies are in harmony with the Head over school philosophy and objectives it is likely that the Deputies' decisions will be compatible with the shared value base and therefore acceptable to the Head. (Bush, 1981, p. 84)

Obviously the Deputy's own perception of the expectations of the Head is as important as the Head's actual expectations. The theme of shared leadership, referred to sometimes as the concept of 'partnership', is suggested as a potential resolution of role ambiguity and uncertainty, and the pioneering course material leaves this notion open for further exploration by other writers.

A major advance in the recognition of the place of Deputy Headship as a significant role in school senior management came with the extension of membership of the two Heads' professional associations to the Deputies. That Deputy Headship lacked a rationale for so long was reflected in the delay in admitting them. Previously, the National Association of Head Teachers (NAHT) and Secondary Heads' Association (SHA) had memberships consisting exclusively of Heads. The National Union of Teachers (NUT) and National Association of Schoolmasters and Union of Women Teachers (NASUWT) both admitted Heads, many of whom held joint membership of an ordinary teachers' union as well as a Heads' organisation. Only the Assistant Masters' and Mistresses' Association (AMMA) excluded Heads, thereby, in true nineteenth-century fashion, emphasising the rank of all teachers other than the Head as being that of 'assistant'. This was in fact the case until the designation 'Deputy Head' was used in the Education Act (No 2) 1986. Since 1987, the NUT has prevented Heads and Deputies from being members if they also held concurrent membership of one of the Heads' organisations. This was intended to prevent a conflict of interest where it was felt that Heads had in some cases seen themselves as representatives of 'the management' and therefore less committed or even opposed to teachers' industrial action.

In addition, the Heads' organisations, while supporting the salary aspirations of the majority of teachers, had started to emphasise the particular demands of Headship and Deputy Headship with concomitant implications for higher remuneration. The NUT was left in the position of having lost a number of its Head and Deputy Head members, while still not excluding those who chose to make that union their only professional association.

Admitting Deputy Heads to the Heads' associations was not the historical inevitability it might be mistaken for. It was thought, and is still thought by many Heads, that Deputy Headship is a very distinct role from their own. If the Deputy is essentially an assistant or go-between, with authority derived from the Head, then the individual's interests are more akin to those of other teachers. They differ from senior management which in this view is vested in the Head alone. After all, the Head is ultimately accountable for the actions of all staff, including Deputies, and has to accept responsibility when things go wrong. In times of industrial action, there had been occasions when Deputies supported staff, for instance, by refusing to take a share in the supervision of lunchtime arrangements, leaving Heads to take full responsibility. The very nature of the Deputy's job always meant that from time to time there was the possibility of disagreement. In the rare cases where this escalated into a deeper conflict, it was thought that advice from different associations would be appropriate.

Another complication in the admission of Deputies lay in the fact that the two Heads' organisations had different types of membership: the NAHT was open to primary and secondary members, while the SHA, as its name implied, was a secondary-only organisation. Deputy Headship in the primary school could be very different from that in its secondary counterpart. The much smaller scale of most primary schools places a greater emphasis on the leadership of the Head alone. Coulson (1976) suggested that 'there can be little doubt that most Heads and Deputy Heads believe that it is the Head's job to set goals for teachers and that he should personally supervise and control their work' and that

'Heads and Deputy Heads consider it appropriate for the Deputy to act in an administrative capacity on the Head's behalf' (p. 42). At another point in the same study, Coulson stressed the lack of significance of the primary Deputy's role in his statement that 'Because the identification between the school and its Head is so close and Heads typically adopt an all-embracing leadership style, little room is left for the development of a distinct rationale for Deputy Headship' (p. 43).

## The search for a rationale

The lack of rationale for the typical primary Deputy examined here reflects a more general problem for Deputy Headship set against the diversity of styles Headship may take. The undifferentiated and crude concept of authoritarian leadership by the Head was still very much a reality in the smaller secondary school, as in the smaller primary school. The larger schools, of both types, were more inclined to develop management structures in which the Deputy Head had a key role. Ten years after Coulson's research, the NAHT (1987) could describe and contrast the roles of Deputies in the primary and secondary schools in far more confident terms:

> With this great growth in the Head Teacher role came a parallel growth in that of the Deputy, once seen as the most senior of the Assistant Teachers but now recognised as a 'Senior Manager' with high levels of responsibility. In secondary schools management by a closely knit executive team is now the norm. Secondary Deputies no longer have narrow responsibilities related to one special area of the school and its work, but are involved across curricular, pastoral and administrative aspects and are clearly 'Heads in the making'. In primary schools, the Deputy is today a partner with the Head in the organisation and management of the school and a 'Head Teacher in training'.

This is an indication of a considerable change in the assumptions surrounding Headship, in a climate in which the expectations laid upon Deputies could be increased, as well as in the assumption that Deputies and Heads could reasonably expect each other to work either as partners (in the small school), or as fellow members of a senior team (in large schools). Some other questions are raised; for instance about the level of involvement in policy formulation of other staff, such as the heads of department as a group in a large secondary school, and how communication to the governors might be cumbersome, if not impossible, in the event of trying to share out the Head's responsibilities for this aspect of accountability. Nevertheless, the statement is a considerable achievement. It confirms recognition of a more sophisticated state of thinking about the role of Deputy by the majority of Heads.

Formal admission of Deputies to the two Heads' associations had now taken place and was well-established by the time statements like the one above could be made. The SHA admitted Deputies in January 1984, and the NAHT followed its example shortly after. In the light of events which were to follow, this seems hardly too soon.

During the course of the 1986 salary negotiations, a serious suggestion was made to reduce to one the number of Deputies in each school. In their leaflet of the same year, *The Voice for Deputies*, the SHA claimed to have resisted this successfully and to have won the protection of numbers as previously defined. The negotiations were an opportunity to define the role of Deputies within the secondary school, and to confirm their responsibilities within team management. It is quite clear that this recognition was achieved at a time when the position of Deputy Head might have been removed altogether, in favour of a less clearly defined sharing of management through a number of staff. The impracticability of administering such a system, and the intolerable stresses it could have placed on Heads, may be guessed at as succeeding chapters here suggest the volume of work required from a senior management team in a large secondary school.

If the SHA has made considerable progress towards articulating a rationale for the secondary Deputy Head, then the NAHT, as would be expected from an association with a more global membership, was seeking, through its specialist working party, to make a statement which provided for similarities as well as differences between Deputies in primary, secondary and special schools (NAHT, *op.cit.*). Similarities between sectors were found in the personal competence required of the individual in classroom skills, 'building and co-ordinating a curriculum team' and 'integrating the school community'. It was emphasised that in the secondary sector, managerial effectiveness was not so closely related to success as a practitioner, although incompetence in this respect indicated unsuitability for such a post. Leadership qualities were identified as a common basis for success as a Deputy. However, managerial and administrative skills should form an accretion around a basis of classroom competence for Deputies in all sectors.

Deputies were divided into two broad categories – the 'backbone managers' who tended to stay in their positions, and the transitory 'Heads in the making'. It was suggested that 'people skills' were an important part of the job, and they had to be supported by management expertise in the following specific areas:

. . .awareness and understanding of schools as organisations; decision
making; counselling skills; meetings; chairmanship; management of
change; interviewing skills (in appraisal, counselling, selection for
appointment, disciplinary procedures; maintenance of morale; resolving
of conflict; team leading; personal organisation strategies; organisational
planning and administration; group dynamics; delegation.

At first sight, it might appear that these skills would be expected
of the Head and of others in the school: for instance, a head of
department would expect to use counselling skills and to maintain
morale. However, sharper definition of the management skills
required of Deputies could distinguish their role from that of Head
as being the 'facilitator' of particular policies and work of groups
within the school. This concept is rather left open for future
discussion, although the necessity of distinguishing the Deputy's
role from that of the Head's when they are working together in
the partnership of a senior team is acknowledged in point 4 below.
The document concluded by summarising six main factors
underlying Deputy Headship and its future development:

1 Being a Deputy Head is a satisfying job in its own right – it is not
just being an apprentice Headteacher. In fact, for some Deputies this
view of their career prospects is an irrelevance, because they may not
wish to become Headteachers.
2 In a modern school with a dynamic and progressive management
style the concept of a senior management team is central.
3 This style of management will be an important element in the overall
ethos of the school.
4 Within the senior management team the Deputy will have a crucial
role to play, one which is not necessarily subordinate to the Head
Teacher (as that idea has traditionally been interpreted) and may be
based on agreed areas of responsibility rather than a delegated list
of duties. This role distinguished from the Headteacher's by the fact
that the latter's authority is rooted in his or her ultimate legal authority.
5 The new management structure also implies a much greater possibility
for Deputies to negotiate and create their roles.
6 In the secondary sector there should be a greater willingness to take
part in job rotation schemes at senior level.

The production of manifesto-style literature such as this indicated
both that the role of the Deputy Head was indispensable to school
management, and that attempts to define it simply would continue
to raise more questions than they answered. However, production
of a statement of this nature demonstrated that the position of
Deputy Head had finally begun to come of age.
     The problem of defining a single rationale for Deputy Headship
has lain in the variations necessary for it to apply to every different

school. The practical duties of the post can only be carried out with authority if they fit within an accepted rationale. Placing them within a recognised framework is important, because the comment 'It's the Deputy Head's job' can easily be made to cover an increasing and unlimited number of minor and major tasks of every description. Negotiation of a Deputy Head role and functions is at one level determined by the structural requirements of a large organisation. These include giving effective leadership and support to the main divisions of the school for which middle managers are responsible, such as heads of subject departments. At another, it is the result of a rather delicate personal chemistry between the Head and other Deputies, in which strengths and weaknesses are implicitly recognised and mutual support of fellow members of the team shapes its internal dynamics and capacity to respond to the needs of the school. For these reasons, this book examines practical tasks of Deputy Headship from a point of view which is both technical and subjective. Methods of taking stock prior to a decision (such as curriculum analysis) are as important to master as is an awareness of the currents of group influence within the school's micropolitical system, when the need for a decision is presented to a staff meeting.

In order to focus upon the way in which major Deputy Headship tasks are allocated, the position is treated as the first point of delegation of responsibility from the Head. For this purpose, a deliberately *bureaucratic* view of management is taken. This has certain emphases, as Bush (1986) points out:

> Bureaucratic models stress the importance of *hierarchical authority structure* with formal chains of command between different positions in the hierarchy. This pyramidal structure is based on the legal authority vested in the officers who hold places in the chain of command. Office holders are responsible to superiors for the satisfactory conduct of their duties. (p. 32)

While this articulates the bureaucratic tendency in its purest form, expressed thus it does help to clarify a number of questions concerning the Deputy Head's authority and expectations to fulfil a *directing* as well as a *negotiating* role. Negotiation may be central to an institution's consultative ethos, but the actual power to ensure that policy is activated has to be exercised through the positional hierarchy of the school.

In this strictly hierarchical model, the Head's unitary responsibility for the functions of the school is first divided through the definition of Deputy Headship duties. A common division between curriculum and pastoral Deputies raises questions about the desirability of seeing the two as being distinct functions within the school. It may reinforce the feeling of isolation or inability to influence events sometimes experienced by teachers holding particular responsibilities within the divided hierarchies, or it can prevent innovations in curriculum when they transcend departmental boundaries. For this reason, the debate about specialist versus generalist Deputy Heads is taken up. However, it is a question which cannot be answered dogmatically, by asserting either that rotation of tasks between unspecialised Deputies gives greater personal satisfaction, or that rotation creates confusion for staff as well as for the Deputies themselves. It depends upon whether or not all tasks are rotated, how often, and the size of the school which determines the complexity of tasks. The question has to be considered with reference to the conditions of individual schools and their structural needs. Chapter 2 outlines the debate and suggests practical arrangements for the distribution of functions.

## Administration in its place

Administration takes up a significant part of Deputies' time. Deputies have to be warned constantly not to allow this to dominate to the detriment of management functions, and it is an important responsibility of those who define Deputies' tasks and allocate functions to be aware of this. A distinction has to be made between routine, low-level administration, such as checking the balance of register totals, and administration of higher-level tasks. For instance, staffing analyses might contain information which remains confidential in the interest of the staff themselves, and a curriculum analysis requires careful checking by the person who best understands the whole school's timetable. In this case administration is at a higher level, and directly informs the types of policy decisions the senior team makes. Of course, register totals are vital pieces of information, but making summaries can be done by an ancillary member of staff so that broad patterns of pupil absence and attendance may be studied by the Deputy.

This is an example of the distinction between administration which is best undertaken directly by the Deputy and that which should be delegated. The other distinction is between administration which becomes a negative force because it overwhelms and obstructs management thinking, and that which facilitates it. For the Deputy, almost as much as for the Head, it is a distinction which must be made in personal self-appraisal, and a methodical approach to this question will be considered in Chapter 3.

A need to develop speedy assessment of the relative importance of different elements of administration is matched by the significance of the extent of which Deputies have to take responsibility for negotiating their own roles with the Head and the staff they work with. Deputy Headship is most in danger of becoming a ragbag of discontinuous minor tasks – in effect, a 'non-job', when the office is filled by a 'non-person'. Against this background, the all-important early months in the post are as critical as they are for Headship. Headship merits its own study in this respect (Weindling and Earley, 1987), and Chapter 3 is of particular importance in accounting for the processes by which the Deputy role is first defined from a subjective point of view, as well as detailing the administrative methods which may be applied to get to grips with the management of the school, including being flexible enough to take account of weaknesses or peculiarities in the Head's way of running the institution.

## Selection and development

Deputy Head selection itself is fraught with distinct problems, including selectors' lack of awareness of the nature of the role; the great difference in the requirements of the job from those which likely applicants will have experienced before in their careers, and the fact that admission to the ranks of Deputy Headship is virtually a pre-requisite for becoming a candidate for Headship later. Chapter 3 is deliberately prescriptive about the organisation and conduct of the selection exercise, intending as it does to lay down guidelines to help those who select Deputy Heads, as well as those who aspire to Deputy Headship.

Once in the post, Deputy Heads need a planned course of professional development as much as any other member of staff. In part, the experience of being a Deputy is seen as a form of preparation for Headship – although this is only the goal of some Deputy Heads. The style of Headship and the way in which team management is developed has much to do with promoting or constraining the career of a Deputy Head. However, the considerable personal responsibility which must be taken for professional self-development means that other measures can be taken when support is lacking. These imply active, constructive responses to circumstances. Cultivation of such attitudes adds to the satisfactions of Deputy Headship and is useful for those who are to become future Heads. It helps to overcome frustration and to maintain a creative approach to school management at times of difficulty for the school. Professional development should include briefings and courses on particular aspects of developments concerning the school, as well as the experience and understanding of as wide a range as possible of the subdivisions of the way it is managed. Chapter 3 also develops this suggestion in depth.

A rationale for Deputy Headship encompasses an acceptance of delegated power, and a provision for negotiation and mutual understanding of roles derived from the institution's particular needs, in dialogue with the Head. Given this, it is then necessary to examine the skills required to work with staff as individuals and in groups. The 'people skills' (NAHT, *op.cit.*) overlap with those of the Head, but are employed in working more with particular middle managers, such as subject departmental heads on the timetable, pastoral heads on individual case-studies, or any other individual members of staff with a particular problem. Skills alone are insufficient without shared values and mutual professional understanding of issues. The Deputy's strength comes through working with others in detail on the examples above, and sharing successes and disappointments felt within the school. Chapter 4 explores practical examples of relationships in action and under test.

Deputies may vary in their own preferred personal style, as do Heads. They bring areas of expertise to a job, as well as personal strength in their ability to cope with particular types of pressures – arising from acute demands made by staff, pupils or the Head. The growth of individuals together in a team, as well as the need for the team to complement the Head, is developed in Chapter 5. This is the point at which subjective tensions, such as role ambiguity and the need for a person of strong individualistic ability to harness it to the benefit of a group effort, becomes apparent. A selection of delegated responsibilities is examined further in the chapter on key tasks to underline the relationship between role and particular tasks which bring the Deputy into contact with pupils, parents, external agencies and the Head.

## Conclusion

The expectations placed upon the Deputy Head are intimately bound up with those which apply to Headship. Deputy Headship in its present form is influenced by historical considerations as well as by the changing nature of Headship, and the development of management structures to serve expanding, more complex educational institutions. A wide variety of bureaucratic and subjective factors, alongside the great variety of needs schools have, go to make the statement of any rationale for Deputy

Headship only of any use if it remains flexible and responsive to different types of schools.

Admission of Deputy Heads to the two main Heads' associations has considerably enhanced the recognition given to the position, even though attempts to arrive at a simple definition of Deputy Headship suitable for all schools still create more problems than they solve.

# 2  Deputy Headship as delegation

Deputy Headship is the first point at which the Head's responsibilities are delegated. The way in which Deputy Heads' jobs are defined has implications for nearly all planned management structures within the school. It will reveal much about the stage of management development a particular school has reached, the Head's skill in defining delegated tasks and the philosophies of education at work. It will also reflect upon the personal qualities and professional abilities individual Deputies are able to offer in their posts and the trust Head and staff feel confident to place in them. In the days of smaller schools, Heads may have delegated strictly limited tasks, such as looking after stationery and stock, disciplining troublesome pupils and giving informal advice to younger colleagues. As schools grew, it was no longer possible for one or two people to cope with the volume of work required.

Two types of delegation then occurred. One used a formal model in which Heads could create a self-consciously rational, bureaucratic structure. It assigned tasks and distinguished between the broad types of functions which together formed an organisational whole. Maw (1977) identifies three starting points for this process derived from statements of:

1 The main objectives of the school.
2 The different groups within the school.
3 The main tasks of the school. (p.97)

From this is drawn the system in which Deputies each lead a middle management team such as the departmental subject heads, and undertake a particular task (constructing the timetable, for example).

In contrast to the formal model, a subjective, personality-based approach was often used. Delegation could be based upon perceived strengths, abilities and peculiarities of the individuals available in post. This assumes that the combined attributes of a team are always somehow adequate for its purpose. Its effectiveness is also dependent upon close co-ordination between Deputies; it is easier to operate within smaller schools.

Divisions of Deputy Headship duties are usually defined in larger schools as relating to middle management structure. They may pertain to one aspect of the school only, or be deliberately defined to cross a number of structures, generating a sense of interdependence between Deputies and Head and simultaneous awareness of current issues as they occur.

The method by which responsibility is then taken for a group or area of work in the school varies. The job may be to service, shadow, or act as catalyst to a middle management group which meets regularly. But even these three very different activities can encompass wide variations in the actual control exercised by a Deputy. Maw (*ibid*) distinguishes between 'those who report directly to the Head on all their major responsibilities, and those who report mainly to an intervening level of hierarchy' (p. 94). In practice, there may be considerable overlap between Head and Deputy, created by the informal and formal access middle managers have to the Head on the one hand, and by the extent to which individuals are in the habit of discussing a wide range of matters with the Deputies on the other. Informal access is often used to overcome the deficiencies of the formal system, particularly to cut across the divisions between specialist Deputies, or when lobbying support for a particular course of action when the Head and Deputies are known to be making a significant decision.

The importance of delegation and Deputy Headship job definition grows when a change of management structure is implemented. Change of Deputy Headship responsibility signals a new importance for a given area of the school. For instance, an innovation such as the introduction of a new form of pupil profiling will concern all staff, but would ultimately be administered by a particular Deputy accountable for its practical realisation.

This sort of accountability emphasises the hierarchical, planned nature of delegation. Trethowan (1983) defines delegation in schools as 'giving a task for which the Head carries ultimate responsibility to another teacher, with that teacher's agreement' (p. 1). In this functional definition delegation to the Deputy Head is no different to that of any other teacher. Unlike other teachers, though, Deputy Heads have to evolve a continuous response to changing circumstances. Being on hand as a 'troubleshooter' can lead to a gradual accretion of unplanned functions, obligations and expectations from staff. They may usefully see authority as shared with the Head, rather than delegated. The danger of overuse of the Deputy should be countered by a periodic review of tasks in which functions can be clarified and made clear in school policy documents issued to all staff. (See Appendix 1 for an example.) These should appear under the signature of the Head, as a confirmation that, despite the indeterminate location of power which occurs within a strong team of Heads and Deputies, ultimate legal authority is still vested in one person.

Delegation often results in specialisation of tasks. This has been seen as a problem, from the Deputies' point of view (Todd and Dennison, 1980), in cases where organisational efficiency is hindered by having a team of Deputies in which each individual only possesses a partial view of what is going on. Rotation of duties (Stone, 1986) is one way in which quantity (if not quality) of experience can be shared. It allows for the development of a form of corporate management in large schools where a team of Deputies is on hand to discuss and decide upon general policies. Its disadvantage is that when aspects of the day-to-day running of the school are totally delegated from the Deputies to various middle management groups, direct access to much information and immediate knowledge of the feelings of staff is lost. There can also be confusion as to where final responsibility for decision-making lies. The advantages and disadvantages of the two approaches will be dealt with fully later in this chapter.

The most common division of Deputy Heads is into pastoral and curriculum specialisms. Todd and Dennison (*op.cit.*) established a continuum of five recognisable differentiations within this split. In Categories 1–3 there is a more or less clear distinction between the pastoral and the curriculum Deputy. This ranges from very strict role delineation with a precise job description, to intermediate positions with flexible allocation of responsibilities, still mainly around the pastoral-curriculum division.

Categories 4 and 5, the other end of the continuum, are characterised by lack of prescribed specific responsibilities. Here, a large degree of co-operation is claimed to exist, and specific responsibility is limited to minor tasks. (The variation in clarity of specialisation is not related by the writers to size of school, although it is suspected that the larger the school, the more necessary it is to articulate the Deputies' roles clearly.) Apart from pastoral and curriculum responsibilities, specialisation may include oversight of Community Education, staff development, girls' welfare, examinations, or taking charge of one particular site in a split-site school. However responsibility is divided for the purposes of delegation, it usually rests upon beliefs in which elements go together to make a school successful. They include theoretical models of management, psychological descriptions of learning and developmental processes, and fundamental social and political philosophies. Whether articulated openly or not, they affect the way in which divisions of responsibility are thought to be possible, and how effectively they are pursued. For examples of this in action, we now turn to the most common designations.

## The Deputy Head (pastoral)

There are two essential functions of the pastoral Deputy Head:

1 To create an ethos of pastoral care in the school (with the Head).
2 To lead a team of pastoral heads or middle managers (either with or on behalf of the Head).

Work on the first function implies a close understanding of the Head's perceptions and assumptions, although it also offers the opportunity to influence them. Ethos means as much a climate of opinion and understanding as it does the acceptance of formal aims and objectives. Creating an ethos is primarily to do with bringing a vision of an educational community to life. Creative imagination and social commitment come first, but the next stage is the clear articulation of basic principles, beliefs and aspirations. These are best conveyed in internal school documents which appear under the Head's signature. Secondary discussion papers may be written by the Deputy Head and others. Examples would include: 'The challenge of underachievement', or 'Developing the system of rewards and sanctions'. They augment and supplement the main policy papers.

At this point, it is necessary to ensure that documentation and official pronouncements are in harmony. The Deputy Head is particularly needed to act as a catalyst for the expression of staff views and receive the feedback which will indicate how far policy can realistically be achieved.

Johnson et. al. (1980) identified seven areas of pastoral work which can be used to assess the comprehensivity of aims and objectives, and the range of concerns with which the school's pastoral ethos concerns itself. They were:

1 To provide a secure base to which the pupil can relate within a large school.
2 To identify and respond to any problems the child is experiencing as an individual.
3 To monitor and regulate the attendance, punctuality, behaviour and progress of each pupil.

4 To systematise the recording and communication of information relevant to the welfare of individual pupils.

5 To make recommendations about special educational needs of individual pupils.

6 To interact with the pupil's home regarding all aspects of pupil performance.

7 To collaborate with the education welfare service and other agencies so that pastoral care within the school and welfare provision and support outside the school complement one another. (p. 21)

Each of the areas identified has a particular relevance to a Deputy Headship perspective which is quite distinct from that of the Head. They require in the first instance a detailed understanding of the intentions of the Head which have been arrived at after consultation and discussion with staff, as well as knowledge of likely staff reactions and a primary responsibility for the administration and set of procedures necessary to make this work.

The formulation and implementation of policy are never separate: area 1, the provision of a secure base, is the most fundamental challenge both to the creation of ethos and to organisational skill. While the Head's task is to decide upon the structure of the system, such as a horizontal grouping arrangement by years, or vertical age grouping by houses, the Deputy Head has a complementary role in establishing:

1 The trust and feeling of security parents and pupils have in the system.

2 The confidence pastoral heads have in their own position and the support they can expect.

Success here will depend heavily upon the quality of working relationship pastoral heads have with their Deputy Head. A detailed perception of the strengths and weaknesses of staff in particular tasks – which may include dealing with parents, coping with incidents of physical aggression, counselling insecure staff about the handling of difficult teaching groups – is important here. The tackling of specific incidents should place as much operational responsibility as is possible in the hands of the pastoral middle manager directly involved in a particular case. The Deputy's job is to monitor, assist and, while working with colleagues, take note of developments with particular implications for the school's pastoral policies.

The planning and development of a pastoral curriculum is one unifying activity which concentrates thinking about what can be achieved, once the creation of a secure, orderly, sound base to which the pupil can relate has been established. It involves creating a programme related to the needs of each age group and taught by the members of staff closest to the personal needs of pupils.

Examples of such programmes have been developed at length by Hamblin (1981) and others.

Unfortunately, many schools have used published material in a way which was never intended. Suggestions for group work were foisted upon unwilling form tutors, who had no awareness or training in how to cope with the classroom dynamics of open-ended discussion work. The prevailing ethos of some schools made this difficult or even impossible for the most experienced practitioners.

Here, the sensitive pastoral Deputy finds ways to give pastoral middle managers the confidence to bring the pastoral curriculum to life in the classroom, and to help teachers develop their classroom technique. This is done, initially, by establishing the needs of children in a particular school, given its catchment area, the most common styles of learning and classroom procedure which exist in the school *as it is* (not necessarily *as it should be*), and considering a practical response. The Deputy might ask of the pastoral leaders one of the following questions:

1 What does a new pupil need to know about the way the institution is organised to get the best from it?
2 What range of skills and knowledge is needed by each third-year pupil to be able to enter into the process of option choice effectively?
3 Are there any common types of conflict situations in this school which we could train our pupils to cope with better?

From the discussion which this engenders, there may come demands for a school-based system which will make use of imported published materials. The need to develop a structured dialogue with pupils about the progress of academic work as well as through the systematic teaching of study skills are two examples where school-produced approaches may be supplemented by additional purchased materials.

The emphasis on building self-confidence within pastoral middle management suggests the particular skills needed to develop such a team. Although it may well report to the Head direct for some or all of its formal deliberations, much of its day-to-day operations will rely upon the Deputy Head both for leadership and administrative support. An ability to deal with problems quickly and efficiently will provide an example, both of personality and procedure, which – if it is right – will be readily picked up by others.

For instance, the Deputy might assist a year head in dealing with an aggressive parent, using tact and reason to draw out the underlying causes of distress, to suggest ways in which the school will try to help in the future, admitting blame or partial blame if it is justified. At the same time, the situation is used to emphasise the role of the year head and comment on possible monitoring of the pupil and future home-school links which will be used to maintain contact over future progress. A number of aspects of pastoral policy have then been actioned in a particular instance. Although the Deputy has resolved a particular problem in person, the methods used will be readily adopted at middle management level – ensuring that responsibility is exercised as far as possible by the person closest to the issues involved.

This example shows one of the ways in which the Deputy is involved in distinguishing reality from rhetoric. Because statements of pastoral care often represent the school's highest aspirations to shape the morality and social standards of its young people, they are inclined to lose touch with reality. From detailed observation of the effects of pastoral care systems in a number of comprehensive schools, Ribbins (1985) reported that staff views usually contrasted sharply with the official statements of the school. In the shortcomings identified, a number of elements of pastoral care emerged as often not really working effectively. They included unclear specification of the role of pastoral middle managers, uncertainty as to who should deal with crises, poor communications generally, and not using form periods for pastoral care.

In part, this list of deficiencies sets an agenda for managing pastoral care in its present phase of development. It also points to those issues which the pastoral Deputy uses to establish contact with staff and pupils, because these distinguish the Deputy Head function from all others in the school. This involves operating in contact with basic individual problems affecting pupils and staff, as well as taking a share in the strategic management of pastoral care. It is through involvement in particular staff problems with pupils that the effectiveness of policy can be assessed. Crises, particularly, can be used to influence more than just the outcome of a particular event. Two aspects of basic care commonly involve the pastoral Deputy in crisis management. These are:

1 Acute disciplinary problems and emergencies with pupils.
2 Emergencies involving staff and parents.

Both require practical, flexible responses, and both require policies which are as much the Deputy Head's job to evolve as they are the Head's.

An example of the first might run as follows: a pupil has been reported as being 'difficult' over the past few weeks by several members of staff. Now, an incident has involved the pupil using bad language to a member of staff in front of the class and walking out. The pupil is found wandering the corridors, and is persuaded by another member of staff to come to the Deputy Head's office to discuss the situation.

The Deputy provides an immediate response to the problem in stressing the seriousness of the offence to the pupil, but also attempts to discover the underlying causes of the current problems. These might include disturbance at home, inability to come to terms with changes in personal relationships with friends, or a general feeling of inadequacy to cope with the level of work being expected in one or more lessons on the week's timetable. While the Deputy will at first handle the problem directly, and even conduct a short counselling session if appropriate, the subsequent management function in relationship to other staff will be emphasised as soon as possible. The pastoral middle manager will be involved in the case quickly, to give background information, if necessary to liaise with parents, and to suggest, in the light of detailed knowledge of the individual pupil, further guidance, monitoring, or setting of a personal contract of behaviour. In addition, the tutor will be informed and, in more problematical cases, the Head.

However, once this example has been dealt with at an individual level, policy questions are raised which are generally up to the pastoral Deputy to answer:

1 At what point should the tutor, pastoral middle manager and Deputy be brought in to deal with individual problems?
2 Is there a clearly understood system of communication and referral for this sort of case?
3 Is the referral system triggered too often, or not often enough?
4 In which circumstances are outside agencies or parents brought in?
5 What happens when a pattern of disruption is associated with a particular teaching subject, teaching space, or teacher?

It is also necessary to keep records summarising the number of referrals in order that an evaluation of the pastoral system's special case load can be made and changing trends noted. This will include details of the number of referrals to middle and senior management, subdivided by year and/or house. Hard, quantitative data of this type is useful in reviewing the pastoral system, both with the Head and fellow Deputies, and with the middle managers. A danger of the pastoral Deputy's work is that the school day starts to present an overwhelming number of referrals and special cases. In part, these expand to fill the time available, and can only be controlled by an insistence that answers to the questions suggested above are based upon a team approach in which work is shared between the Deputy and year or house heads.

This being said, it is also necessary for the Head and Deputies as a team to ensure that in any school of 800 or more 11–16 year old pupils, a rota of senior staff makes one named individual always on call to deal with acute emergencies.

The fifth policy question, centred upon the quality of teaching and learning which the pastoral system is expected to support, has implications for communication between the pastoral and academic Deputies. There is no point in dealing with pupil behaviour problems if the organisation of teaching and learning is inadequate. The example given may arise from a case of that, emphasising the interdependence of the Deputy Head's work and of the traditional pastoral/academic divide in secondary schools.

# The Deputy Head (curriculum)

As with the Pastoral Deputy, there are two essential functions of the Deputy Head (curriculum):

  1 To create a curriculum suitable for the needs of all pupils in the school (with the Head).
  This is to include particular responsibilities for:
    (a)  the admistration of associated resources and staff;
    (b)  assisting in the development and maintenance of a climate of professional opinion and debate in which teaching and learning remain flexible and responsive to changing needs and interests of pupils.
  2 To lead a team of heads of departments or faculties (either with or on behalf of the Head).

If the most comprehensive definition of curriculum is the sum total of all that is going on in the teaching and learning processes in a school over any given period of time, then it includes social and informal learning – the province of the pastoral Deputy. For practical purposes, the organisation of formal and academic education is the main concern of the curriculum Deputy, although this rather arbitrary division of responsibility should not be used to obscure the interdependence of the two positions within senior management.

The responsibilities of the curriculum Deputy have a certain pre-eminence as far as Deputy Heads themselves are concerned. In Paisey and Spackman's (1982) review of *Deputy Heads' Perspectives of their Jobs*, fifty Deputy Heads were asked to rank different areas of decision-making in order for their 'critical importance for the good order and progressive development of the school'. (p.155)

First came 'Staffing' – a responsibility which may be allocated to any Deputy, but is often primarily handled by the Head. The next three categories in order of importance were:

1 Curriculum objectives.
2 Curriculum content.
3 Timetabling/use of plant. (p.155)

Realisation of the first two can only be made through effective operations of the third – itself the most visible manifestation of the way in which power has been exercised and priorities determined in the use of staff across the school. Timetabling is not an end in itself but the administrative function through which curriculum policy succeeds or fails, depending on the extent to which the right people can be placed in suitable rooms with the best possible groupings of pupils.

At one level, the curriculum Deputy would appear to be the most powerful position which the Head can bestow, or person to whom functions can be delegated. Paradoxically, it is because of its importance that the curriculum Deputy experiences the greatest variation in autonomy from school to school. Some heads may construct the timetable skeleton and define many of its constraints, leaving the Deputy to do little more than write up staffing within pre-ordained structures. Others may hand over far more to the Deputy; even total autonomy over staffing and rooming decisions which have a major effect upon the ethos and atmosphere of the school.

The most effective delegation of responsibility to the curriculum Deputy is to hand over a large amount of the administration of staffing and timetabling within policy guidelines which are arrived at jointly with the Head. This does not necessarily mean a rigid division between strategic and tactical planning, or between making management decisions and doing clerical work (with the Deputy undertaking the latter in each case). Rather, administrative detail in the hands of the Deputy should be used to inform, warn, suggest possibilities, and indicate solutions to problems faced by the Head in making curriculum decisions. In these, the team of Deputies, as well as the team of departmental heads, should be fully involved.

Whereas curriculum policy-making in its broadest sense is a responsibility of all school management, a number of particular responsibilities and approaches should be expected from the curriculum Deputy. The development of school-based in-service work dealing with practical aspects of the teaching process is one example. It includes workshop sessions in which any teacher might join:

1 Layout and readability of home-produced worksheets.
2 Establishing a code of procedure with the 'difficult' class.
3 Supporting the slow learner in the mixed-ability classroom.
4 Marking and assessment.

Other approaches, apart from open workshops, include introducing items of this sort onto a staff meeting agenda, working parties, production of discussion papers and reports, as well as one-to-one discussion with colleagues. None of these approaches exclude either the Head or departmental heads from operating in a similar way. However, when the curriculum Deputy has an overall grasp of the administration of the curriculum, it provides a base from which activity can be initiated.

It must be appreciated that the approach of the Deputy Head to curriculum planning involves both the rational, linear aspects of administration and the ability to negotiate with people. Curriculum Deputy Headship involves working in partnership with the Head, acting as middle person, yet taking a personal responsibility for outcomes directly related to organisation. Here it is necessary to identify the more simply defined tasks. Smetherham and Boyd-Barrett (1981) give examples of five identifiable criteria for effective management of the curriculum which may be itemised and checked off at work in school:

1 Does the school have an organisational chart showing the line of curriculum responsibilities for each member of staff?
2 Does each member of staff possess a known and agreed job description?
3 Do different areas of the curriculum possess a scheme of work?
4 What subjects does the school teach?
5 What are the stated aims of the school? (p. 7)

These types of criteria can be used to distinguish the processes about which there must be total understanding between Head and Deputy. They also help to structure discussion with staff when participating in policy change.

If, for example, a new subject is being introduced, or a new division of time between subjects initiated, then the innovation will affect each level of planning separately. Individual members of staff at level 1 may be replanning teaching approaches to cope with an extended range of ability, which leads to an overhaul of schemes of work in level 3. Although the debate should be based upon the school aims of 5, the reaction of different subject middle managers to proposed changes which affect their share of curriculum time favourably is often based more upon self-interest than the altruistic motives related to agreed school aims. This is where the Deputy should be in a position to assess a wide variety of conflicting views from departmental heads, helping them to articulate their positions more clearly, and assisting the Head and senior team to be aware of the likely support for particular courses of action, or what points of contention need to be more fully tackled before a general staff consensus for change can be created.

A method used by Deputies to assist the Head in ensuring that decisions are made in time to be effective at a certain point of the academic year, or for the next academic year, is to generate a curriculum decision chart showing the tasks to be accomplished, and the best time by which to accomplish them. An example of this is given in Appendix 2.

Apart from ensuring that there is a spread of involvement in curriculum debate and planning, a main responsibility of the curriculum Deputy is to ensure that the quality of departmental leadership and internal organisation is maintained and improved where possible. The Deputy cannot be an expert in every subject, but will have the skills to assist heads of department tackle their work:

1 By promoting common principles of teaching, learning and assessment suitable to the school and its catchment area.
2 Ensuring that common policies exist in each department to create continuity of learning between teachers and through years, and to make sure that unnecessary overlap of subject content does not occur as a result of lack of communication.

In realising these aims, the curriculum Deputy will often be closer than the Head to the practical problems involved, and more immediately aware of the climate of staff debate, especially when general, theoretical considerations of aims are tempered by administrative difficulties (real, imagined or deliberately created!) The basic aims are best achieved by following through two apparently contradictory approaches. One is to insist upon a commonality of administrative approach to such requirements as the need for each department to state its philosophy, aims, planned teaching approaches, assessment policy and broad details of resource management in a document of common format. The second is to encourage a creative diversity and individual 'flavour' to each department, allowing strengths to be built upon, and generating the sort of climate to encourage inventiveness and new thinking. This cannot come from heavily prescriptive planning from a centralised management, but will arise in schools where the Deputy adopts an open-minded and encouraging approach to staff to analyse and respond critically to their own class room experiences.

When working on the development of subject middle managers, it will be found that different departmental heads are at different stages of development. Sometimes, this is related to the vigour with which their subject is being debated at national level, and the extent to which the departmental head feels its representative. An example of this was the enthusiasm of heads of Mathematics departments after the Cockcroft Report. Development of the department is also related to the length of time for which the team has worked together, to the length of experience its members have had in the school, and to the standing the departmental head has gained. They may also be at a particular career stage: involved in induction, development, plateau or preparation for promotion stages. Their departments will likewise move through distinct historical phases, not necessarily in this order:

innovation – development – consolidation – peaking – crisis – decay – regeneration.

The Deputy leading a group of departmental heads will use awareness of this when advising individuals or helping them to make departmental decisions appropriate to what can be effectively achieved at a given point in time. Knowledge of strengths and weaknesses will also be used to co-ordinate the departmental heads as a group. Chairing the group may be undertaken by the Head or the Deputy, but the Deputy has primary responsibility for ensuring that members find its meetings mutually supportive.

There should be an opportunity for focusing upon issues which directly concern the group. When other sections of the school are implicated, this should always be noted with a view to its being raised elsewhere or by the Head and Deputies at their own meeting before further action. One healthy function of the meeting is to receive and allow for the airing of complaints and criticisms, another is to raise topics which assist in the development of a commonality .of approach to education. Examples, at different levels of significance, might include:

1 Parlicular aspects of departmental tasks such as report writing: format, style, purpose, and language.
2 Questions relating to pupil assessment in the third year, concerning option choice.
3 The care and guidance of supply teachers within departments.
4 Links between departmental heads and appropriate members of staff in the primary 'feeder' schools.

A further development of the Deputy's leadership of the heads of department is to initiate self-help groups to deal with more specific questions. These may focus upon priorities decided upon by the

Head and senior team, but will be the responsibility of the Deputy to co-ordinate. They may take the form of teach-ins or seminars open to all members of staff, taken by the Deputy, a knowledgeable member of staff, or guest speaker such as a local authority adviser. The groups' aims are best made fairly specific, with a brief to examine and make recommendations upon particular aspects of teaching and learning within the particular school. An example of this in action is when a group is set up with a brief to examine published curriculum materials following a generalised feeling among staff, shared by the Head, that more should be done to raise reading standards in the first three years of the school. In order to create an agenda in which a variety of staff with different interests may share, a number of questions are to be asked about the published materials a range of departments are using, with particular reference to:

1 Readability using a measure of reading age.
2 Accessibility or interest levels based upon the shared subjective judgements of teachers.
3 Value for money.
4 Extent to which new teaching ideas of value are suggested.
5 Setting up further study groups within departments for assessing more specific departmental needs.

Here, the curriculum Deputy is both guiding and generating debate through the participation of staff, rather than managing in a 'top-down' process.

This type of involvement also allows for a subtlety and range of individual staff contribution which does not otherwise come about from the relatively hierarchical meeting of departmental heads alone with the Deputy. The Deputy Head is best placed to chair this type of cross-curricular group, having a whole-school view, based both upon administrative knowledge and awareness of particular departmental strengths, without being in a position to defend the demands of any particular area.

A number of divisions of management functions have been allocated to the Deputy Head (curriculum) in this account, for the sake of clarity. Although individual schools may vary in the emphasis given, it is clear that most tasks cannot be accomplished without very close dialogue with the person responsible for those which are described as belonging to the Deputy Head (pastoral). This applies particularly to assessment and record-keeping, to communications with parents (including reports), and to the establishment of the procedural aspects of classroom behaviour (by teaching staff as well as by pupils). These links will be returned to again in Chapter 5.

## Other Classifications

Although the definition of the Deputy's job is at the discretion
of the Head, and there could be as many different definitions as
there are schools, the most common two types have been dealt
with above. A number of other job titles are found in some schools.
They may co-exist with the conventional pastoral, academic
division, as in the case of 'senior Deputy', or they may represent
a division of responsibility for particular circumstances, such as
Deputy Head (community), especially where school is part of a
community college.

The 'senior Deputy' is designated in schools where one person
is nominated to take charge of the day-to-day running of the school
in the Head's absence. Holding this position is compatible with
any other job description, except one which takes the individual
off the school site frequently, as might be the case with a community
Deputy. In a good team of Deputies, any individual should be able
to take over in an emergency. The danger of designating a 'senior'
is to imply otherwise, although institutions with an ethos
emphasising hierarchy may find it a natural thing to do. Good
management implies that arrangements should be made to cover
possible contingencies such as the Head's unexpected absence.
In this case, the longest-serving Deputy should be the single-
designated person should the need arise. The job of *deputising*
will be dealt with in Chapter 5.

Another title is the 'Senior Master' or 'Senior Mistress', generally
applied to the third Deputy, allowable in schools of Group 10 size
and above. Unfortunately, although the individual has the same
salary as the other two Deputies, use of the title can imply that
the person is the lowest status within the senior team. Many schools
no longer use this title or that of 'third Deputy', preferring instead
to emphasise the co-operative nature of the management team,
in the expectation that a similar approach will be fostered at
departmental and classroom level.

The title 'Deputy Head (administration)' is often given to a third
Deputy, and used as a general term to encompass a number of
functions not undertaken by the others. This allows for a flexible
response to particular needs of the school. It may include such
functions as examination secretary, oversight of buildings and
repairs, health and safety at work, and arrangements for staff duties,
as well as some of the other tasks dealt with in the next section.
At worst, this job can become a mere administrative post without
any real managerial responsibilities. It also runs the danger of being
a collection of tasks which the other Deputies do not wish to
do and have, therefore, allocated to someone else. (Little wonder

that where it exists this post is often undertaken by the most recent arrival.)

The work of the Deputy Head (community) ranges from taking responsibility for all non-school activities within a community college, to fostering community links from a conventional school. In the community college, each senior member of staff may have a specific community responsibility. While the Deputy Head (curriculum) might have a watching brief on adult education in the day and evening, and the Deputy Head (pastoral) make an input into youth work, the Deputy Head (community) will take final responsibility for those operations as well as directing the other range of activities. They will vary greatly in degree between community colleges, depending on the institution's location, stage of development and resources provided to enable it to develop community education. Ideally, the community Deputy should have support and opportunities to develop policies in:

> youth work, adult education, the needs of the retired, unemployed, young mothers and pre-school group.

Community Deputies can be subject to limitless and unrealistic expectations. It is always possible to achieve more, and always tempting to take responsibility personally for activities which ought either to be self-motivated, or dropped. For this reason, it is necessary to be particularly clear about what can and cannot be done. The functions of the community Deputy are:

1 To develop appropriate policies.
2 To determine what can realistically be achieved, given the resources available.
3 To instigate groups and activities which can become self-sufficient after an initial period of support or subsidy.
4 To evaluate achievement and identify needs as challenges to future policy.

A balance between functions should help to avoid the danger of being drawn into servicing an ever-increasing number of activities without additional support and without a methodical approach to ensure that they become autonomous and self-regenerating.

The community Deputy in a conventional school, as distinct from a community college, has a more restricted field of operation, and may combine the community function with one of a number of others. This can include responsibility for parent-teacher association activities, staging school events such as an annual fete or carnival, press relations, and open evenings. As with other areas of responsibility, a record of parental and community contacts over the year should be established in the form of a chart or display.

At the end of the year, it is useful to gather information about the effectiveness of policy by accounting for:

1 The number of events of all descriptions.
2 The number of parental contacts made (including parents seen more than once).
3 The number of parents who have not been contacted or have not made contact with the school.

This role is particularly associated with boundaries between the institution and the world outside. The reaction of parents, reputation with the public, the expectations external groups and bodies may have about sharing in control and policy-making within the school, may all come to the notice of the community Deputy as a result of personal contacts, before they reach the Head and other Deputies. For these reasons, the community Deputy should always be supported by the team, and protected from overwork, if necessary by means of well-formulated policies to community education which have been evolved with the co-operation of fellow members of the senior management group.

Posts are frequently advertised as 'Deputy Head with responsibility for Girls' Welfare'. In the past, a female Deputy was often appointed as junior Deputy to an otherwise all-male team of Heads and Deputies. Her responsibilities in real terms were limited to girl pupils' disciplinary referrals and being answerable for the state of girls' lavatories. The effect of this could be to render the individual concerned marginal to school policy-making, to depress the self-image and aspirations of female pupils and staff alike by depriving them of an effective role model in senior management, and to suggest that girls' welfare was something other than a proper concern of all staff. A girls' welfare designation of the wrong sort, like this, can also produce an inhibiting effect upon the self-image,and hence upon the effectiveness and job satisfaction experienced by the individual. Richardson (1975) comments on the 'sex-linked roles of Deputy Head and Senior Mistress', suggesting the danger of Senior Mistresses finding themselves 'vaguely associated with material caring functions, welfare and counselling, to the exclusion of tasks that have to do with organisational management'. She also points to a common failure in sex-stereotyped senior management roles when 'skills deemed appropriate in a man are often denied to the woman, while those deemed appropriate to a woman are equally denied to the man' (p. 73).

None of this is to deny that certain management functions might be best associated with a female Deputy, provided that they do not involve tokenism. Given that negative discrimination needs to be countered by positive discrimination, useful developments of the specifically female role include:

1 Monitoring of equal opportunities in subject choice and classroom practices.
2 Monitoring career development of female staff, including checks against sex-discrimination in internal promotions and appointments.

Even with this focus, the job of a Deputy determined by gender remains problematical. Its designation may be associated with reactionary or progressive views of gender roles within the institution. With the long-term improvement of attitudes and eventual elimination of sexist assumptions, abolition of this designation might be possible.

# Day-to-day administration: bringing policy to life

*Administration* and *Management* are two distinct but interdependent elements of organisational processes in school. The former is to do with the practicalities of running the institution, including keeping records, controlling finance, requisitioning stock and following up building maintenance, while the latter concerns essential purposes and policies. Administration takes up a large part of the Deputy's daily working life. Although described by many as a 'chore', the parts of administration which involve holding and familiarity with information and records give the Deputy a unique source of power and expertise. In practice, administration is also never fully separated from other aspects of management.

For instance, each time a list of parents' evenings is drawn up for the year and issued, staff reaction – positive and negative – will be made. It may provide a series of questions and challenges to school policy regarding home-school links.

At the same time, administration by Deputies, as far as most staff are concerned, represents their most visible contribution to the running of the school. Being asked to cover for an absent member of staff, or being told to move room to make way for a practice examination, may be unpopular as requests in that they disturb the habitual functioning of the individual, but being given wrong information about where to move or being sent to the wrong room to cover, is likely to lead to a general questioning of authority by the individual who is unlikely to make the nice distinction between administration and management. Administration can be used both to foster and to obstruct policy: it is not unknown for

Deputies to find ways of making certain actions a priority, and of quietly dropping others.

For example: a new system of diagnostic testing of pupils after primary transfer may be nursed through carefully by a Deputy who believes in its value, with staff having protected standby time and secretarial assistance to present a report on their findings. An ill-conceived scheme of options within a particular department, leading to excessive pupil movement within the lesson, disturbing other groups, and using a more favourable than usual pupil-staff ratio, may find itself impossible to timetable for a second year running, however much the departmental head insists upon the scheme's success and believes it had the backing of the Head. Despite the power conferred by administration, Deputies are always in danger of being involved in 'overload', taking on new work, without fixing proper priorities for what is undertaken. One of the best ways of establishing deadlines, and the relative priorities various types of task must take at different times over the school year, is to draw up a termly calendar of major events showing such items as school trips, holidays, parents' evenings, report deadlines, staff meetings, governors' meetings, school plays, and school concerts. The calendar should be agreed by the Head and Deputies in the first instance; contributions from staff to be added, and then published. In this form it becomes a useful bureaucratic device.

A number of other administrative tasks assist in the creation of a sense of order and ritual which generates security for staff and pupils alike. Drawing up a break duty list involves more than a clerical function: it means placing people where they can be used to best effect, pairing less experienced with more experienced staff, and putting them in a position from which feedback can be obtained about the behaviour of groups of children in the school grounds and early identification of particular safety hazards.

Taking responsibility for reporting building defects and repairs may be used to monitor the state of different parts of the school buildings, including the incidence of vandalism and its association with particular groups, times of day, or teachers.

A system of filing and follow-up at set intervals should be used. In cases where the building is unsafe, and should not be used by pupils or staff, the recommendation should always be made in writing and copies kept for future reference (see Appendix 7).

Making arrangements for the cover of absent staff is one of the most sensitive aspects of daily administration. It is a task which should be seen both as an exercise in managing people, and one requiring detailed record-keeping, especially in schools where staff absence is high. Priorities in the use of staff time must be established by the Head and Deputies as a group and be communicated to staff. Without support for a simple, workable system, the Deputy is again in danger of being left with unrealistic expectations – both to protect staff from being excessively called for cover, and to provide cover for absence due to illness (as well as for every other good reason judged to be so by the individual in question!)

Records gathered in the course of covering staff absence should provide information for the Head about the absence patterns of particular members of staff, as well as the staff as a whole. They may indicate the need for individuals to be given further help or professional counselling, or be an indication of general trends in staff morale. In both cases, an apparently routine administrative function provides an important source of information for management interpretation and judgement.

All Deputies should be in a position to store documents dealing with policy areas for which they are responsible. These include syllabuses, schemes of work, reviews of pupil performance, pupil set and group lists, staff appraisal documents, and records of meetings. A sound, basic administrative system is more than often found to lie behind a clear-headed contribution to policy-making in the senior management group.

# Generalist or specialist?

Divisions between Deputies will always seem rather arbitrary where the Deputies actually work together closely. They will also raise questions about the basic principles involved in separating aspects of school management, whether along the lines of pastoral and curricular functions, or having a separate manager for different sites in a split-site school. Each school will work out for itself how far it wishes its Deputies to be specialists or generalists, or whether or not rotation of tasks is desirable. There is no single best way of doing things, but the most effective solution will depend upon the circumstances of the individual institution and the quality of its self-anslysis, quite apart from the unique strengths of its Deputies as people. It is useful to conduct this analysis alongside the arguments for and against specialism. Here are some of the main considerations:

## *In favour of the generalist*

1 In most schools there is more than one Deputy. This allows for a team approach to management.

2 The Deputies need to be able to advise the Head on policy-making across a wide variety of issues. For this reason, each Deputy needs a 'whole-school view', rather than a partial understanding which comes from specialist responsiblity for particular areas of the school.

3 Generalism helps to overcome rigid divisions elsewhere in the middle-management structure. If, for instance, there is a focus of attention on pupil learning processes in the classroom, then the separation of pastoral from curricular structures is irrelevant.

4 In the day-to-day running of a school, there are many occasions when a member of staff needs to make immediate contact with a Deputy Head. Rigid demarcation would lead to frustration and delay.

5 The effect of individual staff change at Deputy Head level is less disturbing to the functioning of the management group.

6 Generalist approaches allow the individual Deputy Head a fuller experience of all aspects of the school's management functions and form a better preparation for Deputies seeking promotion to Headship, as well as making it easier for any one of the Deputies to substitute in the Head's absence.

### In favour of the specialist

1 Specialism has advantages which do not necessarily rule out many aspects of the generalist contribution to a senior management group.

2 Staff need to know to whom to turn for assistance with matters requiring a degree of specialist knowledge, for example, the 'statementing' of a child under the provisions of the 1981 Act concerning Special Education.

3 If one Deputy is the point of reference for particular tasks, then one individual will feel responsible for following through a problem, avoiding the possibility of wasteful duplication of effort.

4 Certain tasks essential to the running of the school require considerable expertise. The experience of constructing a timetable builds up a stock of knowledge and understanding of problems which is helpful in future years.

5 Without a working, in-depth knowledge of important areas of the school's functioning (such as examination entries, rooming, primary-secondary transfer, record-keeping etc.), power is transferred away from the senior management group which gradually ceases to have the facilities to ask appropriate questions, to hold individuals accountable for their work, and to be able to make changes. Specialism locates accountability for a wide range of functions within the compact, practical working group of the Head and Deputies more effectively than does generalism.

Given the advantages and disadvantages of pure forms of specialist and generalist Deputy headship, it is desirable for a mixture of approaches to be adopted. The 'mixture' approach allows for several advantages:

1 The senior group can act as an extended information base and source of advice from which the Head can take decisions, or as a fully informed decision-making body in itself.

2 Clarity of responsibility for aspects of school management is still retained.

3 The job of Deputy Headship in itself remains interesting for the individual involved, who, while possessing specialist expertise, is called upon to take part in activities affecting the complete range of school life.

4 A 'mixture' approach, properly adjusted to a particular institution's needs, can allow for rotation of tasks over a period of years, without loss of stability and expertise from the senior group.

If extremes of specialism are to be avoided in Deputy Head job definitions, then the extreme solution of constant rotation of tasks is equally unsatisfactory. A compromise is to arrange a phased rotation of tasks. This must be based upon a full articulation of all work undertaken over a year by members of the senior team. It can then be subdivided into three distinct levels of task, comprising those which can be shared or duplicated as part of everyday management teamwork; those which can be rotated annually if desired, without an appreciable loss of efficiency, and those requiring significant expertise in which experience or personal contacts involved are such that it is better only to exchange tasks after three or more years doing the job. Examples of tasks allocated to each of the three levels might be as follows:

## Level 1 (tasks easily shared and duplicated)

1 Dealing with immediate pupil crises, and school patrol.
2 Induction of new staff, and formal staff appraisal.
3 Organisation of parents' evenings.

## Level 2 (annual change is possible)

1 Liaison with parents' association.
2 Arrangement of daily substitution for staff absence.
3 Supervision of teaching practice students and liaison with local initial teacher education institutions.

## Level 3 (these tasks should usually be undertaken by one individual for at least three years

1 School timetable.
2 Responsibility for the pastoral or curriculum middle management team, and chair of team meetings.
3.Primary/secondary transfer and liaison with 'feeder' schools.

# Conclusion

To make a rotation system work effectively, it will be necessary for the Head to negotiate changes in tasks with the Deputies, firstly as individuals and secondly as a group. The results of this negotiation should be communicated to staff, and allocated responsibilities for each year should be printed as a section in the staff handbook. The larger the school, the more complex the process of delegation will be. A methodical approach to this is a primary task in establishing management *structure*, which should be done not in the abstract, but with reference to the school concerned and people involved. This chapter has outlined considerations common for most large schools to be taken into account when negotiating the work of Deputy Heads. It has also suggested steps by which the functions of Deputy Heads can be established within an interdependent team. Establishing senior management functions with clarity is a difficult and time-consuming process. A school which can do this successfully is likely to be successful in accomplishing its many other important purposes.

# 3 Getting started

Promotion to Deputy Headship involves far more than even the best prepared individual is likely to expect. It is a major step beyond being a head of department or year, mainly because it suddenly compels the post-holder to bring a whole-school perspective to the way in which problems are seen. An assiduous head of department will quite naturally examine any proposal for change from the point of view of the department – its contribution and standing within the school – rather than make a detached judgement on the whole school about the compromises needed in one place to achieve redeployment of resources to another. To do otherwise would be to appear uncommitted. A newly appointed Deputy who moves from one school to another ends one term in which appointments, capitation and pupil numbers within one section of the school may amount to an obsession. At the start of the new term in a new job, countless simultaneous demands are faced from every specialist department; trivial individual needs and enquiries demanding instant decisions present themselves, together with the challenge of teaching in a different catchment area which would confront any teacher new to the school.

At the same time (as with Headship), the post is relatively isolated. It is not really understood by parents, governors, and many staff and with the common lack of definition of what is expected, there is a need to adapt to a set of expectations and responsibilities far more diverse and ambiguous than anything encountered before. Making sense of conflicting demands, to be a credible part of the intellectual leadership of the school, as well as being capable of sorting and processing a share of routine administration, requires a robustness of thought about what can be expected from experience as a Deputy Head. This is best developed well before applying and being accepted for the post. The purpose of this chapter is to suggest a strategy of preparation, selection, induction and development. It is intended to be used by Deputy Heads themselves, by appointment boards, and by those who work most closely with them – their Headteachers.

# What prepares people for Deputy Headship?

Most deputies will have spent at least twelve years as classroom teachers, about four of which will have been as successful middle managers. As movement in the teaching profession slowed down throughout the 1980s, so there was a trend to appoint older people to senior positions. For Deputy Headship, the age range considered suitable is still between 32 and 45. Many selectors seek individuals who will serve energetically as a preparation for Headship, which means that sufficient time must be allowed them to acquire experience before making Headship applications in their forties. Experience outside teaching, in industry, or in an education system abroad should also be considered an advantage rather than a handicap. Similarly, the importance of ensuring that a balance of women are appointed to senior positions means that quality, not just quantity, of experience should be taken into account when considering candidates who have taken time out from their careers to have children.

Experience of more than one school is important in establishing balanced views and the sense of judgement required in the job. Where circumstances of career have not allowed for this, every opportunity should be taken to visit other schools. Work as a visiting examiner or moderator, as well as involvement in inter-school extra-curricular activities and sports, are two useful activities by which experience can be broadened. Different schools have different management styles, ethos, curricular and pastoral structures – each with their own strengths and weaknesses. The ability to assess them critically, and to speak from experience, helps to generate the self-confidence needed to participate with others when entering an established and experienced management group.

A Deputy's own performance as a teacher in the classroom is the first judgement which staff make and provides the initial basis upon which respect is gained for other dealings. Although the post requires a less than average teaching time commitment and demands a range of skills beyond excellence in the classroom, ability as a teacher still forms an essential pre-requisite. The way in which personal presence is used to control or resolve a difficult situation with pupils; habits exhibited of good lesson-planning; practical knowledge of methods of tracking and recording the progress of learners, as well as the tendency to be a person to whom pupils can turn naturally for advice and counselling, all count: they are needed as a foundation for someone who will provide a role model for other staff. Insecurity at this level has potentially damaging effects upon the quality of work at others, and should be considered before assessing other contributions from the individual.

As we saw in the previous chapter, Deputy Heads in larger schools generally lead or assist in the administration for a particular group of middle managers. A successful track record as a subject or pastoral head enables the Deputy to understand the needs of this group. A head of department with a difficult member of staff – perhaps a habitual absentee or a person who fails to mark pupils' work – will find it easier to discuss what should be done with a Deputy who has also faced similar challenges when serving previously in the same position. At the same time, a pastoral or subject head who wishes to become a Deputy should also plan to acquire a broader insight into school management.

Well-prepared candidates will have expanded their understanding of management issues through short courses in particular areas like pastoral care, timetabling, or appraisal. Part-time postgraduate qualifications such as the Open University Advanced Diploma in Educational Management are another way to gain a thorough grounding of theoretical knowledge. Reading of literature and awareness of recent legislation affecting education indicate an extended range of professional interest. While staffroom colleagues are sometimes dismissive of too much theory for its own sake, the future Deputy must be sufficiently aware of current theoretical debates to be able to articulate clear personal educational principles, against which school matters can be considered in a logical and unprejudiced manner.

New Deputy Heads bring with them the experience, successes and failures of their previous school. Their assumptions about the role will reflect their own past experience of Deputy Heads and the Head they have worked under. Their most important preparation for the post lies in their previous experience of daily school life. In this, it is useful for the successful subject or pastoral head to examine personal areas of weakness, or lack of close operational knowledge: the departmental head of the large 'core' subject such as mathematics, for instance, might need to gain an insight into the process of third-year option choice for the fourth- and fifth-year curriculum. This reveals the problems of matching pupils' choice to available resources as well as the inter-departmental pressures and internal politics facing smaller departments, and requires the involvement of the guidance programme with pupils and their parents at this stage of their school career. A person whose post is primarily pastoral may extend professional knowledge by examining aspects of the school's curriculum in more detail. One exercise is to use all non-teaching time available to 'shadow' a particular pupil or group of pupils throughout a day or week. This allows for an examination of the range and nature of learning experience offered to pupils by the different departments. If time makes this form of exercise impractical, then a survey of all written work from a particular tutor group over a week can produce much specific knowledge about how pupils are performing, as well as allowing incidental observations of marking and assessment practices in action.

A way of gaining knowledge and experience of key processes within the school is to volunteer or ask to assist with a relevant task: helping to timetable by running rooming checks of the finished document, or undertaking the rough draft of a complete section of the timetable – say the sixth form, or years one to three only, is one method. Taking charge of daily substitution for staff absence over a period is another way of working alongside a Deputy Head for substantial blocks of time, giving an insight into the school's timetable, as well as staff absence patterns and ways of coping with them. It also gives an opportunity to deal direct with staff across the school – sometimes to find ways of persuading them that covering a class, though unpopular, is necessary!

Organisation of examination entries with the examinations secretary or responsible Deputy Head helps both to lighten the load of someone undertaking an onerous task, while providing an opportunity to examine the range of entries, subject choice, variations between subject entries by pupil gender, and to understand school policy on examination entries. Simple statistical examination of the percentage of pupils studying a subject who are finally entered for it at examination level, as well as the percentage who passed it when entered the previous year, is an exercise which others might not have the time to undertake. The figures obtained reveal much about the policies and effectiveness of particular subject areas (and may have to be handled with discretion).

Another part of the desirable track record of an intending Deputy Head is a record of successful involvement in particular projects. Introducing a new syllabus at examination level, or developing profiling approaches in the first year, are two examples. Innovations should arise from carefully analysed needs in the school, and be seen through. In the past, rapid promotions were often gained by individuals who had been involved in national curriculum projects during the early 1970s. More recently, maintenance and consolidation of innovation has come to be seen as being even more important than the original act of innovation in itself.

The choice to work with parents or deal with the public should always be taken. Involvement in a parent-teacher association, or taking a share in the organisation of particular events such as careers evenings, socials and school open days, also help the individual to develop skills which will be important as a Deputy. Above all, future Deputies should have achieved consistently good inter-personal relationships, not only with the team they have taken charge of at middle management level, but with other colleagues across the school. Here, a sense of humour, as well as the ability to keep calm when circumstances are stressful with pupils or other staff, can serve to demonstrate other qualities which are as important as all the rest of the individual's experience and training.

Although there is no limit to the range of activity which can help people in preparation for Deputy Headship, initiative will often have to be taken to secure opportunities unless they are fortunate enough to work in a school with a positive programme of staff development which will encourage individuals to gain experience ready for the next stage of their career progression. Sharing of management tasks will do much to enrich the school in which the candidate is presently serving, as well as helping to maintain personal motivation at a stage when change of job is being actively considered.

## Selecting Deputy Heads

As we have seen above, a candidate for Deputy Headship should have acquired an especially broad range of experience and have demonstrated a quality of professional expertise leading a subject department, a pastoral team, or other significant activity within a school. Nevertheless, selectors are still faced with people planning to make a career jump almost as large as that to Headship, who are largely untested as to the scale and magnitude of the job for which they are applying. When selecting Heads, they are at least able to choose from individuals who have been Deputies, which will have given them a chance to observe at first hand someone working under the pressures of the job. Other responsibilities to be faced are that future Heads will be drawn from the ranks of Deputies, and that the effective functioning of a school's present Head can only be ensured by a strong Deputy or Deputy team. It is necessary, therefore, to know something of the motivation and background of applicants and to understand the personal experiences and processes they go through before arriving on the shortlist for interview.

In a very competitive field, there is a great difference between individuals assessing themselves as being prepared for this particular promotion and being actually selected for it. From the ranks of aspiring Deputy Heads, appointment boards will be considering two main types of candidate and appointee:

1 People who fortuitously fit a given need at a given time. They will appeal subjectively to the selectors through personality, shared prejudices, or whim. They may also provide a replacement for the outgoing incumbent with as little upheaval as possible in the present school. Skills, attitudes, and even teaching subjects offered are compared with what has been offered in the past, and future change is largely discounted.

2 People whose basic educational philosophy and principles are matched with good administrative skills and adaptability. They are likely to be able to analyse the needs of the school they are joining through rational frameworks of judgement derived from experience, belief and consciously acquired management training.

It is possible by chance to become a Deputy Head from the first category of applicant, although with increased competition, and the tendency for would-be candidates to study industrial practices of career development for executives, many individuals aspire to the second. For them, the decision may involve making a highly organised series of application throughout the country – or a considerable part of it.

In this case, there is a need to be aware that a highly professional applications campaign is often at the mercy of a less than professional selection process at the other end. Careful record-keeping of the stage various applications have reached, filing of details of posts, and the rewriting of a basic application letter to suit the requirements of each post must all be managed patiently through a period which may involve inevitable disappointment.

Whatever the discouragement and uncertainty, applications should be made systematically, and with professional judgement. Each set of job particulars should be checked for the particular qualities and experience being sought. One vacancy might require a person with a proven track record as a head of department with the ability to innovate and help a school replan its curriculum. Another may need a consolidator rather than an innovator. The person required will find ways to fit in to existing systems and become part of any already successful operation. While this distinction might appear rather simplistic, many schools require a mixture of both professional personalities to consolidate and innovate simultaneously. Here, the wording of job specifications should be checked to test how far the school advertising the post seems capable of defining its objectives in making the appointment.

The fact that the applicant does not exactly match the requirements of a post should not be a deterrent to making an application, but a study of details should at least reveal special requirements, where extra reading and personal research might be undertaken to consider areas of weakness and the extent to which the individual would feel comfortable in adjusting to them. Examples include schools which have a strong commitment to mixed-ability teaching after working in an institution which is banded or streamed. Multi-ethnic schools, community colleges, and schools with special education units all make specialised demands, depending on the institution and its pupils.

An applications process which may spread itself over many months can be turned to advantage as part of the personal preparation for the post which will eventually be occupied. If a large number of details of posts are sent for in order to make selective returns, then a file of details collected will contain information on varying types of school management structures, different types of Deputy Head job descriptions, school staff handbooks, local authority procedures and so on. Their requirements may help an applicant to sharpen perceptions, improve the letter of application, and to consider further development in a present post. Information on a local authority's policies gained from an unsuccessful application and interview in one case might provide a valuable background if invited back later for interview in another school within the same authority.

Letters of application should demonstrate some of the qualities the individual will be required to show in a senior post. Information should be clearly conveyed and laid out, with decisive, succinct sentences. However, Deputy Heads (like Heads) should be more than mere managers in an industrial and commercial sense: the sort of people they are and the values they represent are as important as the procedural aspects of what they do in the job. Hence, the letter should contain an indication of the individual's basic beliefs in education and processes of teaching and learning. What is said should also be meant. This section of the letter of application should yield the most probing and thought-provoking questions from a good interviewer later.

Selectors must both attract a strong field of applicants and choose effectively from it. However, the evidence about their performance in selection of Headteachers suggests that much of what Morgan, Hall and Mackay (*op.cit.*) found in their study is likely to apply equally to methods of selecting Deputies: further particulars often fail to give an adequate job description and account of related appointment criteria.

Questions were also raised as to how individuals are trained for the post apart from the 'exigencies of the career path' (*ibid*), and 'the extent and accuracy of both lay and professional selectors' perceptions of what the job is about' (*ibid*, p. 8). We have seen above how potential Deputy Heads can prepare themselves systematically for responsibility and demonstrate evidence of this on an application form. Selectors need to consider a number of basic criteria for their approach to the composition of shortlists from this information if they are to make maximum use of the large number of applications for a much sought-after position.

After a preliminary reading of letters of application, the quality of the available field can be assessed and a decision be made as to how rigid or flexible the requirements for the post should be drawn. For instance, will only candidates in the age range from 35 to 45 be considered? Is the holding of a higher degree or advanced qualification significant? Should only candidates with experience in a designated community college be considered for a post involving community education? The extent to which these limitations can be imposed will depend upon the range of expertise on offer. In drawing up the long shortlist, the candidate who appears exceptional or original may also be added. (There is no predictable production-line route to Deputy Headship.)

References should always be taken from people with a knowledge of the candidate's performance in the classroom, as well as of their ability as a middle manager, performance as a member of a team of other middle managers, and ability to relate to their Deputy Head in the school of origin. Other references should at least confirm the conclusions of this single crucial document of professional assessment.

In recognition of the major importance of Deputy Headship, it is usual to give at least two days to the appointment procedures. These should be conducted with as much care as that given to the best practice in Headship appointment, and the interview days should be planned down to the last detail. Nothing is worse than a school demanding the ultimate in administrative efficiency from its Deputy Headship applicants only for them to be treated to a disorganised or hurriedly arranged programme. A day's timetable of events should be issued to candidates in advance. Apart from opportunities to see round the school while teaching is going on, to talk to pupils and staff, and to study additional school documents, candidates should have the opportunity to gain further personal impressions of the institution by meeting staff in small groups. Initial interviewing can be conducted by having one or more small panels of three or four interviewers meeting single candidates in rotation. This can be arranged where six or more candidates are invited on one day. It is rare to invite less than four or more than twelve candidates for initial interview. Where the larger number is desired, an alternative method of initial interview is to invite three or four candidates at a time over several days. This is usually only possible if the local authority is prepared to leave initial selection to the Head. It makes the first stages of selection less tense, and allows for impressions to be gained at relative leisure before the intensity of final interviews. However the interview programme is managed, the host school should always aim to provide candidates with a professional experience valuable in its own right. It should learn from their reactions, and make opportunities to receive feedback about their impressions of the school.

Where Deputy Head candidates are to be questioned by a number of people, including governors, local authority officers, advisers and the Head, it is important that a planned sequence of questions is agreed upon. Internal rivalries and political tensions disrupt the effectiveness of the interview process. At this stage, it is helpful if the Head or officers involved can persuade less-skilled individuals to form themselves into small groups for the initial selection. Final selection should be the reserved responsibility of as small a senior interviewing panel as possible. This saves candidates from being subject to disorganised sessions. At the same time it allows interested parties to participate in the interview process by asking detailed or esoteric questions which can best be responded to in the more intimate atmosphere of small-scale initial interviews.

Much can be learned by arranging for a group of intending Deputy Heads to meet together with staff at an evening reception. This enables senior staff such as heads of department to test out their own perceptions against the experience of candidates who themselves are usually practising middle managers in other schools. It also presents an opportunity to see how candidates relate to each other. While such an event can be criticised for placing an additional pressure upon candidates at a stressful time, it does allow for a chance to get to know them outside the formal confines of the no less stressful interview room. Staff are far more likely to be supportive of a person whose appointment they have had the chance to observe or even participate in.

A selection should be made, finally, based upon the cumulative impressions gained, and as a result of planned questioning about the particular qualities and requirements of the post. Some possible questions are suggested in Appendix 3. But even when all planned processes have been completed in a rational and orderly way, a subjective judgement has to be made about the rest of the team of Head and Deputies. Will the person complement or detract from the balance and interdependence of personalities within the existing group? How far should this consideration be paramount in making the appointment? If, on the other hand, it is felt that a fresh injection of expertise is needed to shake the existing team out of its complacency, then how far is it fair to use an individual in a new Deputy Headship appointment as the vehicle of these intentions?

These considerations make it clear that the relative balance of power held by various individuals involved in making a Deputy Headship appointment will vary greatly from institution to institution. They will also involve extremes of appointments procedure, from the smooth executive-style approach of the well-structured interview programme on the one hand, to the ragged chaos of personal or political rivalry on the other. In one school, the Head will have the main say as to whom s/he wishes to work with. In another, the Head may be forbidden to speak until a final decision is made. The candidate on the receiving end may have to tolerate much. Selectors can save themselves much distress by talking to each other about how they intend to reach conclusions, deciding on the positive qualities they seek in a candidate and resolving destructive tensions in advance.

Finally, the professional value of the interview experience for unsuccessful candidates is confirmed by making provision for each one of them to be debriefed after the interview by a local authority adviser or the Head on the strengths and weaknesses of their application and interview performance. A good candidate will keep a diary of interview experiences, and note down questions asked. This will both help in self-assessment, in preparation for answering questions at further interviews, and be useful in considering the interview process from the point of view of a potential future selector.

## Induction, pitfalls and successes

Taking over as a Deputy Head is very different from assuming charge of a subject department. In many schools, aspects of administration essential to their smooth running, such as daily cover for staff absence, are undertaken by the Deputy, and must be undertaken by the replacement individual from day one. A new incumbent must learn fast and learn alone. Help from the Head and fellow Deputies may be given freely, but the whole-school responsibilities of the post mean that the close, intimate support derived from a departmental or house team is not so readily available. This can make the task of trying to learn the job while retaining credibility in the eyes of the staff more difficult than in any other position, except that of newly appointed Head. For this reason, induction of Deputy Heads should be carefully considered both for the good of the individual and of the institution. It should be regarded as a shared responsibility of the Head, local authority and, above all, the individual. A number of steps can be taken to prepare for taking up the post before the eagerly awaited date upon which a new contract commences.

First, enquiries should be made to find out what documentation (if any) exists, and the following specifically requested:

1  A list of all staff by name, and indication of responsibilities held.
2  Timetable, and timetable summaries or curriculum analysis.
3  Examination results, by subject.
4  Description of pastoral structure and system operating.
5  Staff handbook.
6  Map of school with rooms and room number system.
7  List of ancillary and office staff names.

A useful exercise, in the weeks or months of waiting to take up appointment, is to memorise the names and responsibilities of staff. Much of the meaning of the contents of items 4 and 5 will have been explored already during the selection process, but further questions will emerge in the course of pre-appointment visits to the school. Where it is nearby, a number of visits of an informal kind may take place at odd times when release can be secured during the day, as well as to evening functions. At least two formal, briefing visits should take place at this level of appointment, even if travel for some distance is involved. At this point, a further exploration may be made of impressions gained at interview, and particular problems of structures or individuals which the school may have felt unable to reveal at an earlier stage should now be explored. This is not to say that it is good practice to hide important details of a job from candidates or to mislead them, but many schools, if they do not have 'skeletons in the cupboard', have local difficulties with individuals or departments, which are only known about by those actually in the institution.

Part of the visit should include the opportunity to conduct an initial review of the tasks and people for whom one is responsible. The Head should talk through the middle management team for which the Deputy will take responsibility, giving personal impressions of the strengths and weaknesses of different individuals within it, and indicating a broad view of its future, and whether or not changes or developments are envisaged. For instance, a pastoral structure might be remodelled to take account of expected changes in the school's number of forms of entry, or to utilise particular experiences of the new Deputy.

Now, it is also vital to establish as far as possible a timetable of events for the next year, and for the forthcoming term in detail.

If a single major task such as option choice or timetabling is to be undertaken, then advance research and planning should be done. This will help to ascertain how far awkward issues or processes are going to be left to the newcomer to manage.

The attitude taken to self-induction is the most important of all for success. A good Head will give every assistance, but a Head who is tired or out of touch will not be able to help, and alternatives have to be found. It is informative to ask each member of the middle management team to meet to discuss their work and give a briefing on major school needs as they see them. This sort of meeting takes place best on 'home ground' – in the departmental or year head's office, rather than the Deputy's. Particular requests for future help or hopes for special projects can be broached at this early stage.

In the first week of an appointment, it will usually be necessary to prioritise administrative tasks, whatever well-laid plans have been made in advance. 'Leave it with me' is a useful phrase to utter when trying to cope unsuccessfully with a wealth of detail and a host of unfamiliar procedures. But there must be a system of noting down deferred decisions and requests for information, which can then be cleared in the evening or at the weekend. The establishment of a filing system (on a scale not encountered in any previous job) will constitute an immediate challenge, as information and correspondence arrive in great quantity. If a suitable system does not already exist in an easily understandable form, then a running file should be built up of all that needs to be kept for future reference. Subsequently, a series of categories can be established to cope with future business.

Much more than in a previous job, the Deputy will encounter and work with ancillary staff, caretakers and secretarial assistants. It is vital to become known by and get to know this group of staff. Their co-operation is often more crucial to the administration of the school than that of the teaching staff.

Finally, the period of induction is one of rapidly changing impressions and events. Mistakes and misjudgements will be made, but there will also be unexpected pleasures and revelations. Here the keeping of a daily diary entry of personal reactions and judgements can be helpful when undertaking further promotion in the future, as well as in self-assessment of achievement made and the stages by which it occurred.

There are many pitfalls of Deputy Headship, and they are most likely to be experienced in the early stages of the job. The problems of working with an uncommunicative Head – for whatever reason – have been mentioned. A quick recognition of unofficial systems of patronage or favouritism helps to avoid the tension involved in attempting to provide rational solutions to irrational problems. A person to be treated with great care is the failed internal candidate a successful external candidate has to work with.

At this stage, while a wealth of detail is being processed, it may be difficult at first to gain the co-operation of staff in producing information, revealing timetable details and admitting to the whereabouts of records on individual pupils. All these frustrations must be overcome with patience. In some cases they may well reveal structural deficiencies. Perhaps no-one has real, categorical responsibility for the keeping of pupils' records. Real decision-making for timetabling might have been allowed to become too decentralised into the hands of departmental heads, with the result that timetable changes are negotiated privately without the involvement of the Deputy. Rebuilding structures of accountability and communication cannot be done overnight, and will need the understanding and co-operation of the Head if they are to be tackled effectively.

A new Deputy will also be under test by staff who send problem children to the office at difficult times. Immediate responsibility here is inescapable, but so too is the need to see that staff observe the school's normal referral system and are reminded of it in cases where it has been forgotten – deliberately or otherwise!

Within the first month, newly appointed Deputies should be able to feel some of the elements of success in the post which will make it rewarding in the long term: they will have felt a growing rapport with the Head, and the ability to share thoughts and decisions about day-to-day matters, as well having started to discuss common ground on points of educational principle. They will be able to confirm other senior staff members' impressions of the strengths and weaknesses of the school, and share in plans for its development. It should be possible to say that one is known by most colleagues even in a large school with eighty staff or more, and to have made an initial encounter with many of them. A sense of the pupil intake and the surrounding community will be starting to develop as a background to which initial meetings with individual parents, governors, or others in the community start to take place.

## Career development of the Deputy Head

Deputy Heads proceed through a number of stages of career development, often without realising it. Whether they intend to use the position as preparation for Headship, or develop over a longer time scale, without deliberately seeking promotion, it is important to recognise phases of personal and career growth. With this knowledge, it is possible to measure performance against what should be expected, to undertake new tasks with self-confidence, and to develop personal management skills.

After the induction stage dealt with above, a Deputy Head with eighteen months' to two years' service starts to recognise that some tasks seem onerous chores, and others have become enjoyable. There has been sufficient time to get to know people, and revise initial impressions and judgements. At the same time, it is beneficial to apply a degree of self-analysis. A professional interview with the school adviser is one way to reflect upon achievement and need. Another way is to set aside time specifically to share the Head's appraisal. Some schools adopt an appraisal process in which Heads and Deputies evaluate each other's performance over a set period of time, as a complement to appraisal at other levels throughout the rest of the school. If there is an atmosphere of trust, then a frank exchange of views can help, both in improving performance, and in general day-to-day working relationships.

Although the opinion of a respected professional colleague is always of great value, a number of questions can be considered about performance by noting factual information concerning routine which may in itself suggest areas for improvement. An analysis of time spent over different periods on different types of task reveals actual priorities as distinct from those believed to be in existence. Contacts and approximate time spent can be analysed as follows:

### Over a week:

Record all contacts with the Head, parents, pupils and outside agencies which have taken up more than five minutes to deal with.

### Over a month:

Record all meetings, both formal and planned and the sort of unplanned meeting with middle managers, advisers and ancillary staff which have taken twenty minutes or more to complete.

Data gained from this exercise can be classified using a lettering system to assess how far time is utilised effectively. A possible system is as follows:

a) Useful and necessary contact.
b) Task could have been better delegated or forseen and avoided by proper advance planning.
c) Task took too long, and could have been speeded up by the Deputy having been given a better knowledge of the problem in question,

or better organisation at a simple level – say by organising a filing cabinet better.

d) The contact was effective in achieving its aim.

e) The task should have been immediately and tactfully deferred.

f) The task should have been referred to another Deputy or other member of staff in the first place, if the school's recommended procedures had been followed.

g) The task was accomplished by the appropriate Deputy in an efficient and entirely satisfactory manner.

This systematic analysis provides a background against which decisions can be taken about longer-term career objectives: it identifies strengths in individual work, which for the Deputy might include practical knowledge of particular procedures such as examinations and syllabuses, having detailed knowledge and contacts with the community pupils come from, or gaining a following and loyalty from a particular group of staff who do not necessarily feel total commitment to the Head's wishes on certain issues.

Further stages of development include undertaking specific, more ambitious tasks and directing innovation within the school in the form of particular new projects. At first, this could mean rearranging the system of care for students on teaching practice. Later, it might include undertaking all outline planning and feasibility studies for a major change, such as the development of six-form consortium common timetable with a group of neighbouring schools.

The most important phase of maturity in a Deputy Head career occurs when it has become possible independently to maintain the support of *groups* in the school as well as *individuals*. Obviously, there are times when this may be lost as well as regained, but when a point has been reached at which it is possible to identify which groups will feel able to support a particular action, it is easier to be accepted as a sensitive manager, and to avoid conflict before it occurs. An example would include knowing who will support a change in option subject configurations on the fourth-year timetable. Another is being certain that staff affected will support a degree of internal disruption brought about by a decision to encourage form tutors to accompany their tutor groups for residential education experience.

This is the stage at which the Deputy has become accepted. It does not matter now whether the individual is using the post as a transition stage, or is to become a long-established Deputy: staff have reached the stage at which they can rely on a person to advocate their cause, to supply reliable information about school policy or a special decision, to feel supported, and be willing to give support in any instances involving difficulties with pupils or their parents. Another important advantage now is that it is also possible to gain the 'feel' of staff reaction sometimes more accurately and in advance of the Head. This puts the Deputy in a position of strength and responsibility for interpreting staff mood and expectation. There are times when it even places the Deputy in a position of being a successful apologist for the Head's mistaken actions, making it easier for the Head to reconsider a bad decision.

The notion of mobilising the support of groups has political dimensions, and the extent to which it is significant may depend upon the style and expectations of other aspects of the school's life. If the school is heavily dependent upon bureaucratic procedures and ritual, bargaining about the pros and cons of a decision is of less importance than when a high degree of staff discussion and involvement is customary. In most schools, recognising the existence of what may be loosely termed 'political' influences is as important in becoming an effective Deputy Head as is administrative efficiency.

The need for in-service training to be assessed both in connection with the needs of the individual and the needs of the institution applies as much to Deputy Heads as it does to Heads and to other teachers. However, special demands are made by Deputies. They are relatively few in number: though there are more Deputies than Heads, they are fewer than the ranks of middle management. They have the advantage of not being so potentially isolated as Heads in that there is always more than one Deputy in a large school. But they do not share the advantage which a good team of heads of department have in being able to support one another at a forum to express views and exert pressure, as well as enjoying the support of what is normally a subject-based local authority advisory team. In fact, the nature and organisation of advisory teams can create uncertainty in itself: many advisers obtained their posts as promotion from middle management level, and so they have not experienced Headship or Deputy Headship. School Heads are often linked to a subject adviser who also has a general pastoral responsibility for the whole school, but the Deputies find themselves without an adviser to refer to specifically, being subject instead to the interventions of advisers – helpful or otherwise – on behalf of the Head and middle management. Although generalisations are difficult, advisers, because of their characteristic career paths, are less likely to have practical experience of Deputy Headship, however willing and supportive they try to make themselves.

This poses the question: who is best equipped to assess the career needs of Deputy Heads, and competent to train them? Obviously, Heads themselves, or some advisers with experience of the post or a wide experience of working with Deputies on pastoral programmes or curriculum analysis will provide the most useful immediate contribution. Much can be provided through Deputies working together to assess their own needs and to share good practice through a Deputy Heads' support group.

Heads with an understanding of the need may suggest that Deputies consult with others in neighbouring schools with similar roles. The focus of a half-day visit could be to see a particular curriculum innovation in action, or to study an administrative procedure at another school. A Deputy who has changed from a manual to a computer-assisted method of arranging cover for staff absence, can demonstrate and explain the system to a colleague from another school with a candour and frankness which would be difficult to retain in a public meeting. This, like many issues, is sensitive, and involves difficulties which Deputies are more prepared to admit privately to each other than in the presence of an adviser from the local authority. The use of different systems of keeping records on pupils – their admission to the school, progress through it, and the monitoring of behaviour – are all more effectively studied on the job, in a real setting with a person who is actually using them, rather than on a course.

Deputies meeting together discover both profound similarities and dissimilarities between schools. For instance, the timetable process for a faculty-based school, using mixed ability and blocking large portions of a year group together at once, offers a great contrast to the streamed school with differential routes for pupils and distinctions between individual teachers as to the groups they may or may not teach. They also discover, and explore – diplomatically – differences between Heads' enthusiasms and beliefs in their various schools. The most valuable part of this type of exchange is that it confirms common challenges, difficulties and satisfactions in the job, but it also prevents Deputies from becoming parochial as far as their own institutions are concerned. This helps to retain critical judgement upon events going on in daily working life, as well as to continue to ensure that other working practices are viewed with an open mind.

A formal way of extending the help which Deputy Heads can give each other is to set up a Deputy Heads' group at the local teachers' centre. The regular Deputy Heads' meeting at Coventry Elm Bank Teachers' Centre is one example of a group which has met successfully over a number of years. Such a group, while relying upon the helpful contribution of the advisory service, is best served by electing its own officers, planning its own programme, managing its own finances and organising a programme of social events where there is a demand. It should meet regularly – once or twice per term – and be recognised as one of the ways in which school management can be improved by self-initiated activities. Its programme should be carefully designed to motivate people to attend: an emphasis on practical issues and current topics should be mixed with longer-term planning considerations within the authority's schools or the national perspective. Examples of practical issues might include the response being given to a particular round of industrial action, or a discussion of the authority's policy on suspensions and exclusions of pupils.

Where the group is clearly showing its worth, a further development is to stage a conference which may become an annual event. With the agreement of school Heads and the authority, a weekend conference extending from Friday afternoon or morning and going on over Saturday, allows time for a theme to be explored in depth. This is also a good point at which, finance permitting, a nationally known speaker may be invited to address the group. Topics need to be well-judged in their appeal, and timed correctly in the school year. Examples to demonstrate the range include:

Curriculum analysis and accounting methods.
Developments in examining and examinations.
Equal opportunities (for staff and pupils).
Computers in adminstration.
Preparation for Headship.
Staff appraisal.
The management of time.

Each one might form an option within a conference. Some topics like 'the management of time' can be dealt with more fully at a weekend conference along with other aspects of administration such as computers. A suitable guest speaker from industry might provide a provocative stimulus for certain topics.

Other tasks of a Deputy Head's support group can include organising social events welcoming newcomers to the area, and announcing news, from farewells to promotions. As a support for Deputies being inducted, mere attendance can be helpful, although the development of more structured support for newly appointed Deputies could start here by pairing the new Deputy with another experienced colleague in a similar role within another institution.

Another valuable form of support for Deputy Heads has been established by the professional associations and unions. One example is the series of conferences in 1983 and 1984 organised by AMMA. Speeches and discussions were minuted, edited and written up in booklet form for wider distribution among members (AMMA, 1984). Distinguished speakers, including Heads, Chief Advisers, and the Association's own officers, spoke on specific

Deputy Head issues. Such a conference is bound to deal more in generalities than in sharply focused local issues in which people who know each other well already produce well-channelled responses, but it has the advantage both of fielding a larger number of experts than a small-scale gathering can afford, and of allowing a free range of both general and specific questions to be tested against the speakers' reactions and the reactions of a large group of other Deputies from around the country who will approach specific difficulties with a fresh mind.

## Conclusion

We have seen in this chapter that Deputy Head appraisal and career development pose specific challenges, not the least of which is that many persons in authority have only a partial understanding of the needs involved and what should be done. Most Deputies have the support of their Heads, who themselves will almost all have had experience of the role. Nevertheless, it is necessary to realise that a great deal of the process of induction, self-appraisal and arrangements for in-service training has to be self-initiated. Deputy Heads, recognising this, can do much to help themselves through organised local initiatives. If at times frustrations arise through working in a context where problems seem little understood, then this state of affairs is at least shared with fellow Deputies and, of course, the Head, who is frequently in an even more isolated and exposed position when a difficult course of action has to be faced. A realistic set of expectations for performance, and a planned development by a self-motivated individual, is an important recipe for success in Deputy Headship and, it follows, for the success of a team management approach to running the school.

# 4 Working with people: managing people's jobs

## Individuals, groups and the Deputy Head

Job descriptions, advertisements for vacancies, and internal school documents refer to the 'role of the Deputy Head'. The word 'role' is used to mean many things. It implies much more than mere fulfilment of functions and completion of tasks. According to Hunt's (1981) practical management definition, 'A *role* combines the cumulative formal, technical, informal, and personal expectations about a job' (p. 57). From the point of view of Deputies there is a need to look beyond formal 'role definitions' to the variety of expectations placed upon them. These may well be contradictory, reflecting the views of competing groups within the school. This is demonstrated by particular incidents. Suppose that some minor damage has been done in a room during mid-morning break. Three members of staff have different views of the role of the pastoral Deputy, each of which influence their expectations:

1 *The caretaker* wants the group to be banned from the room, and thinks punishment should be administered by the Deputy who is seen as the main dispenser of sanctions to maintain order. The caretaker must be mollified while a course of action is considered.

2 *The Year Head* sees the Deputy rather as a senior assistant detective, highly practised in forensic skills and able to identify the hand behind the majority of graffiti in the school. Subsequently there is an expectation of support for the year head's use of the incident as an extension of Social Education by emphasising to the pupils that responsibility and privilege are interdependent. The expectation is that the tutor group based in the room will have to take constructive action to repair all damage and exert social pressure to prevent its recurrence.

3 *The Head* has recently decided that far too many incidents are being referred directly to the Deputies, with the result that their managerial role in staff development is being constrained. For this type of incident, the Deputy's involvement is only justified if it is used to assist the year

head and form tutor in developing their skills within a planned structure.

In these examples, a close understanding of the role systems at work within the school is necessary to judge other people's assumptions, their reactions to particular ways of dealing with issues, and the expectations placed upon staff. Each case here presents a challenge: the role must be confirmed or denied by what is done. A strong Deputy ensures that role definition is kept under control. A weak Deputy's role becomes merely the sum total of other people's expectations – without negotiation, control or influence.

Roles are played out in schools with their distinctive atmospheres and unwritten rules which define how the Deputy may or may not act. The most important variation lies in the acceptance, insistence or denial of hierarchical modes of relationship in the school's formal structures. A new Deputy has to gauge this, although one promoted from within the school is likely to take it for granted.

Two extremes can be identified, though institutional customs in most schools mean that the majority lie, for practical purposes, somewhere in between, with different individuals taking different attitudes. For instance, in a school where the Head and Deputies are essentially passive and reactive, we find the following:

1 Departmental heads decide on staff allocation to all teaching groups. Cross-departmental teaching and the Social Education programme are extremely difficult to organise.
2 Pastoral middle managers operate a totally devolved referrals system for pupils, control sanctions, meet parents, and file individual pupil records. It is very difficult to monitor the abilities of the first-year intake, to use reports to assess the quality of pupils' progress, or to gain co-operation between the pastoral and departmental heads.

These extremes of habit and custom are highly restrictive to the Deputy Head's room for manoeuvre, and diminish the degree to which the school is actually 'manageable', especially when middle management is otherwise particularly active and well-motivated. The opposite tendency is equally limiting where:

1 Departmental heads expect their timetable to be worked out for them in detail, and provide no assistance in recommending staff for particular teaching teams in different year groups.
2 Pastoral middle managers take little initiative in dealing with individual pupil problems, and refer numerous individuals to the pastoral Deputy. Record-keeping and administration, including register-checks, are always done by the Deputy, who is also blamed for the continued behavioural misdemeanours of more 'difficult' pupils and classes.

These are examples of either an extreme lack of hierarchical role expectations being received from 'above', or the excessive imposition 'upwards' of rigidly hierarchical assumptions. They remove the possibility of the Deputy Head working in partnership with staff, as well as a view of school management in which the Deputy works *through* and *with* people to achieve results. The need is to avoid such undesirable extremes through an awareness of role systems in each school and find ways of consciously regulating the particular pressures which generate polarised reactions.

In Chapter 2, examples were given of the essential functions of different Deputy job definitions. If delegation takes place through the Deputy Head to middle managers, then the formal hierarchical model of management described requires consensus about 'the main objectives of the school', and 'the main tasks of the school'. In practice, such consensus rarely exists in a stable, predictable form within a school staff. It is the Deputy Head's job to deal with and interpret both the goals of group leaders and of individuals within the groups. Group leaders include those who lead opinion within formal as well as informal settings – such as the departmental meeting on the one hand, and the staffroom on the other. Individuals in groups are linked by common subject background, but they may also be linked by gender, generation, political allegiance, union membership, or common interests and hobbies. The Deputy Head needs to be aware of such links, because dealings with an individual are generally reported back to the group and affect future transactions as a result of the esteem in which the Deputy is held, or otherwise.

Here are two cases in which individuals place their own interpretions upon actions and generate unpredictable reactions for groups:

1 The Deputy Head is a former Head of Special Needs. Faced with a reduction on the total school staffing strength of half one member of staff, a decision is taken not to replace the Special Needs member of staff who is leaving. However, a member of the English Department with an appropriate additional qualification is anxious to change the direction of the school's policy to Special Needs. The proposal is to work across a number of groups, 'supporting' the learning year, rather than withdrawing them from the mainstream.

The Deputy is identified as influencing the Head's decision not to replace the vacancy, in order to promote a particular philosophy of Special Education. In addition, the Deputy's espousal of mixed-ability teaching and record of strong union support over the last few years, mean that a known 'progressive' stance is interpreted by the present Head of Special Needs as 'left-wing' bias.

Another member of the Special Needs Department is on very good terms with the Vice-Chair of the Governors. A subjective view of events inside school is quite likely to be reported back in great detail! In this situation change will not be easy. The circumstance most to be avoided is any possible charge of administrative error when calculating the timetable teacher-period input (see Chapter 6).

2 There is a rule that any pupils involved in physical violence must be temporarily excluded from school until they can be seen with their parents. Generally, this does much to preserve the atmosphere of the school, which is situated in an inner-city area. However, one member of staff is constantly reporting pupils to the pastoral Deputy for fighting. The colleague in question has close friendship with a group of older staff known to be opposed to the pastoral Deputy's tendency to counsel pupils before applying sanctions, and advocacy of teaching approach in the classroom as being the primary point of control. In a particular case, after questioning other pupil witnesses, the Deputy decides a reported incident is not sufficiently serious to warrant exclusion. The member of staff who reported it is informed. The pupil's form tutor is told of the outcome (by the pupil), and informs other staff. The staffroom is divided between those who believe that discipline is becoming weaker in the school, on the one hand, and on the other those whose principles favour the style and practice of the Deputy in question.

In both cases, a role is being constructed and defined. Judgements are made about educational principles which are never simple, often controversial, and always inescapable. They show the need to be constantly aware of staff reactions, as well as the individual and group power-bases within school.

Teachers gauge how close the Deputy is to the Head. Whether they do it correctly or not does not matter – their perception of the relationship regulates the attitude they take when trying to influence a course of action. Although Deputies are known to lack the ultimate authority of the Head within the institution, staff will have their own beliefs about the extent to which the Head supports the Deputies, and the influence different Deputies have with the Head. This is more pronounced if one particular individual is always seen to be in the company of the Head, or if, at the other extreme, it appears that the Deputies have apparently no visible social or working relationship with the Head whatsoever.

The Deputy's pivotal position in the distribution of power continues to be through detailed administrative knowledge, including rooming, the distribution of 'difficult' classes on the timetable, the power to determine the pupil composition of teaching groups, and willingness to give support with classroom disciplinary problems. Over these issues, staff feel less threatened and able to be more open in dealing with the Deputy Head than with the Head. They can use the Deputy as a sounding board for new ideas of their own, to test out challenges to assumptions they believe the Head to be making, or to clarify a case they wish to bring to the attention of the Head or an influential working party. Many disputes and disagreements between staff will be brought to the Deputy for arbitration, only going to the Head in a few cases on appeal.

As we saw previously, one example of the testing of individual and group relationships is when individuals are being asked to undertake a change in the balance of teaching time between two subjects. This can often happen if a school is subject to falling rolls, or a reduction in the amount of time allocated to one subject is decided upon in favour of another. It is a test of the way in which the individual has been approached and considered, of the actual room available to manoeuvre given limited staffing resources, of the understanding among staff generally of these limitations, and of the willingness of influential group leaders to accept or support the change. It may well be an occasion where the effects of a badly handled personal negotiation by the Head can be ameliorated by the Deputy. Prompt action can deflect the first line of negative criticism away from the Head by undertaking initial negotiations while a newly introduced idea is thought about by those affected. Deputies need to be aware that they can single-handedly create feelings of resentment, defensiveness or beleaguerment in a group. They can also mobilise support for themselves in a way which builds up a stock of goodwill to assist in future actions.

## The creative role

In some schools the Deputy Head has no formal responsibility for negotiating the work of middle managers. They report directly to the Head through formal events in the school's calendar such as departmental heads' meetings. Particular issues like staffing or the needs of individual teachers are dealt with on a one-to-one basis in the Head's office. The Deputy is only involved subsequently as an administrator (when a timetable adjustment is required) or in taking the place of the Head (when a parent insists upon seeing the Head personally but the Head is not in school).

In this passive setting, Deputy Heads negotiate post-holders' work largely by default. They react to events and decisions rather than initiate them. Proper delegation, of the sort suggested in

Chapter 2, means a clear responsibility of Deputies for their middle management teams. As a result, they will be involved in all background discussion needed to clarify the aims of innovations proposed before they are ratified by the Head. Accepted review procedures across the institution allow for groups to articulate collective goals, and for individuals to explore personal career objectives. Having Deputies responsible for each section of the school's activities allows the task of knowing each member of staff well to be made more feasible than when everything is channelled through the Head.

The creative role develops in an atmosphere of trust and co-operation between Head and Deputies, and between Deputies and their respective middle managers. Their relationship must allow for pastoral and subject heads to make observations and suggestions about the running of the pastoral system and subject departments. This also applies to dialogue concerning the school's more general aims, as well as everyday procedures including the way particular classes are taught or individual pupils have been treated. The Deputy's involvement in two-way communication about the quality of school life lets staff criticise the Head and Deputies if they feel they should. In addition, the personal strengths and weaknesses of the head of department or pastoral team can be talked about frankly. Further consideration is made of performance appraisal later in this chapter.

A capacity to build up the confidence of people in their own capabilities is needed. Access to resources to give support of time and occasional finance from a special projects fund is also required. It involves development of personal counselling skills on the part of the Deputy, who should be in a position to back up advice with action.

There is a very delicate balance between the exercise of a degree of coercive authority exercised on behalf of and in consultation with the Head on the one hand, and the establishment of a mutual recognition of professional authority between colleagues on the other. This recognition is the point at which the Deputy's authority develops independently of that of the Head. It relates less to the hierarchical position occupied by the Deputy in any diagrammatic representation of the school's management structure, and more to the trust established through links, alliances, track record of effectiveness in emergencies, and daily interactions which a Deputy uses to cultivate standing with staff. It must also involve the exercise of intellectual skill and possession of a large amount of up-to-date information, including examination syllabuses, knowledge of how other schools deal with their management problems, local authority policy, and the law. These are but a selection of the elements of background requirements when negotiating the work of individuals by Deputy Heads.

We now turn to the Deputy's work in dealing with occupants of two important middle management roles.

## The pastoral middle manager

If asked about their work with pupils, year heads and house heads can quote the statement of aims contained in the school handbook, but their approach to practical problems needs to be constantly renegotiated and supported. If they have the opportunity to talk frankly with the Deputy about their concerns, then it will prevent a gulf growing between 'official' policy and actual practice. Experienced staff are also able to influence and change policy through discussing their work in a regular review. When considering a pastoral role, it is useful to focus upon any areas of frustration and consider strategies for improvement. Questions about the everyday organisation of school life provide a starting point when the pastoral head considers them:

1 What do I do when my own class is interrupted by another teacher having a problem with one of my pupils?

2 What is my specific knowledge of my pupils' performance in subjects where I have not had the opportunity to see them being taught or take them myself?

3 What further guidance do I need to give my tutors about the use of tutor time?

4 What contact have I had with parents – at school, through home visits, telephone or letter – and how successful are these in accomplishing my intentions?

5 Are assemblies being used to best advantage? Could staff and pupils be better involved and how?

The responses to these questions form an opportunity for reflection and self-evaluation on the part of an individual. If desired, a list of areas for special attention can be drawn up with the Deputy, and reported back upon at the next meeting. These should arise naturally in the course of formal review, but, in the case of more diffident staff, could be raised by the Deputy to encourage individuals to be open, even when criticism of the Deputy and Head could be implied. For example:

1 Are there acute cases of dealing with individual problem pupils in which you have felt that you lacked support?

2 Could the system of record-keeping be simplified without reduction in essential quality?

3 Are you receiving sufficient information about your pupils' learning progress to be able to discuss their work sensibly with them whenever reports are issued, or profiling is taking place?

4 Are you getting enough time to perform your role effectively? Can you give an analysis of how existing time is used, and how you set priorities for performance of tasks when time is limited?

In smaller schools, the process suggested here might be undertaken by the Head. However, it is useful for the Deputy leading the team of pastoral middle managers either to be present with the Head at the review, or to undertake a preliminary interview with the individual to help prepare a presentation around the agreed main areas to be looked at. Where the Head is unwilling to undertake such a formal review, it may be injudicious to set up such an obviously closely defined event in people's minds, but many of the questions can be explored in a series of informal contacts. There is then nothing to stop the Deputy noting down responses and collating them at intervals to assist in the process of review.

## The curriculum middle manager

Curriculum middle managers usually work in a far more established role than their pastoral counterparts. They are helped in constructing their own goals by the fact that most secondary school teachers are trained in narrowly defined subject areas and their allegiances formed in university, polytechnic or college days. Examination syllabuses, the organisation of the school timetable, and the existence of professional subject-based organisations such as the Association of Teachers of Modern Languages all help to define performance objectives both of the department and of individuals within it, quite apart from national curriculum objectives.

Despite this background, tradition has sometimes been more of a disadvantage than an advantage when a school tries to establish consistency in policy for teaching and learning processes. Departmental heads need specific school-based guidance in what HMI (Wales) (1984) identified as five broad overlapping categories:

1 Routine administration and organisation of the department.
2 The planning of pupils' learning experiences.
3 Monitoring and evaluating the work of the department.
4 Professional development within the department.
5 Liaison with other departments, with the pastoral staff, the senior management and with outside agencies. (p. 3).

A starting point for discussion is to examine, with the departmental head, examples of records kept on a particular group's progress and planning notes for particular lessons. This will lead to a general consideration of the degree to which a unity of purpose is established with members of the departmental team about learning styles, organisation of resources and suitability of assessment methods.

For the departmental head, as for the pastoral middle manager, a number of questions might arise from a preliminary discussion with the curriculum Deputy. They focus upon the skills of curriculum leadership, and may indicate areas where the Deputy can help with specific advice:

1 Is there a departmental handbook with clear advice for the new teacher on methods, resources, assessment, teaching style, and how to obtain support when in difficulties?
2 Does the scheme of work for each year take account of the needs of pupils of all abilities and attitudes?
3 Does departmental documentation exist to represent the department's work clearly to pastoral middle managers and staff outside the department?
4 Is the theory and practice of the subject openly discussed at departmental meetings in terms most staff understand?
5 Are all departmental meetings subject to a clear agenda, well-chaired and directed, to the mutual satisfaction of those who attend?
6 Is the administration of the department efficient, clearly understood by all involved, and properly delegated where desirable?

These questions are formulated to allow a Deputy Head without expert knowledge of subject content to understand the processes at work. They also help the departmental head to relate the subject to efforts by the school to establish consistency of policy in matters of classroom style, whole-school approaches to marking and pupil assessment, and to aspects of individual staff appraisal.

HMI (Wales) (*ibid*) are clear that:

The extent to which departments undertake a more systematic evaluation depends to a considerable extent on the expectations of the senior staff, and in particular the existence of a clear whole-school policy which offers a framework within which to work. The direct involvement of the Headteacher or one of his (sic) Deputies in the evaluative process can provide an incentive for the departmental team to formulate their own criteria. (p. 13).

The relationship between the curriculum Deputy and the team of departmental heads differs from that which they may have with the Head. Much negotiation will take place over staffing, timetabling detail, requirements of pastoral middle managers for information on individual pupils and groups of pupils, and the form in which it comes. This access to the specific details and problems of departmental daily affairs gives the curriculum Deputy a unique insight and ability to relate to departmental heads' needs in a way which the Head is unlikely to have time to achieve.

## Appraising performance in partnership

The negotiation of roles is not a single event, but a constant process within the school, as is the definition of pastoral and curriculum goals. As it goes on, the question of how effectively goals are being realised raises itself. Whether one area of the school or the individual responsible for a particular area is the focus of appraisal, the Deputy responsible should either undertake the appraisal alone, or in tandem with the Head. The method of appraisal proposed here is not a top-down, but a two-way, interactive process. Just as in the negotiation of roles an individual may identify areas where more support is needed from the Deputy, so appraisal should present an opportunity for the departmental head or pastoral middle manager to state clearly how they feel that improved performance on the part of the Deputy would improve the school's management.

Much has been written about appraisal and the different forms it may take. In their booklet, *Whole School Evaluation and Staff Appraisal*, Slater and Long (1984) identify three distinct ways of collecting information to obtain:

1 Quantifiable data.
2 Self-evaluation data.
3 Interpretive/Illuminative data. (pp. 10–12)

All three are involved in the negotiation of roles, but appraisal requires that a frank judgement be made of effectiveness – made at given intervals and communicated to the people concerned. The most common form of appraisal is by annual interview, based upon job descriptions derived from the overall objectives of the school. Lyons and Stenning (1986) give one of the best accounts of this system, placing it in the general context of staff planning and staff development. Whatever form of particular school operates, the Deputy Head should have a clearly defined role.

Slater and Long (*op.cit.*) suggest that 'Where the decision is taken to use appraisal interviews as part of the process then a prerequisite must be classroom observation' (p. 12). To this end, the Deputy should always undertake practical observation of the classes in action. This applies whether visiting a particular department to observe its work, or sitting in on registrations, tutor group meetings, assemblies and Social Education lessons in a particular year group or house. A further development of this approach, and one which will be accepted by staff as less inquisitorial, is for the Deputy to be working alongside staff. It may be to help on a particular project such as diagnostic testing of a group within a subject lesson, or taking a special session in Social Education. It should be made clear, however, that one purpose of the visit is for the Deputy to gather data for appraisal, and that there is nothing to stop staff being appraised at the same time to pass on their observations of the Deputy's effectiveness with staff and pupils over the same period.

The expectation here is that the Deputy is able to take greater personal risks than the Head in practical involvement with classroom processes, especially where an innovation or new method of working is being tried. At the same time, the Deputy has authority and is looked to for support. It means that the Deputy adopting the right approach to appraisal is less likely to be seen as a threatening and intrusive figure once careful approaches to the establishment of trust have been put into action.

## Fostering innovation and target-setting

Deputies should be apprised of proposed innovations, and involved at an early stage in assessing the likely effects one department's innovation is likely to have upon the rest of the school. As goals are set and the appraisal process become part of a school's accepted procedures, so should the setting of specific targets for achievement over short-term time spans. New proposals should always be tested to see if they fit in with the school's goals or run counter to them, or whether they require that senior management should reappraise goals at a more fundamental level. This would clearly be the case, for example, if a department was proposing a new course involving streaming or setting in a predominantly mixed-ability school.

Middle managers usually need help in translating rather generalised wishes to innovate into achievable action programmes. A move to source-based work in history away from 'up-front' instructional methods of class teaching might be frustrated by individual staff who appear to accept change in departmental meetings but will not alter their style in the classroom itself. Here, the target might be better achieved in stages. Particular sections of the syllabus could be worked upon in the first instance with departmental meetings concentrating on the assembly of materials and specific advice on their use, and follow up visits to classrooms being undertaken by the head of department to ensure implementation. It is better to set targets which can be implemented successfully in phases, rather than grand plans which fail because early preparatory stages are mishandled or resisted at the first sign of difficulty.

At other times, it may be necessary for the Deputy to explore the lack of targets, or their setting at too low a level of expectation. This is especially true where learning outcomes are concerned. Examination results provide one source of data which may indicate that the wrong syllabus is being studied for the pupils in the school, or that the wrong methods are being used. They also indicate differences in performance between teachers, provided the results are treated with care, and consideration is given to previously existing basic differences between groups.

Targets may also involve plans which should be reconsidered because:

1 If delayed for a few months, they will fit in with a whole-school or LEA initiative. There is no point in one year group starting its own profiling system if a proposal is about to be made for a school-wide system.
2 The department has already introduced a number of initiatives, and is in danger of suffering from innovation 'overload'.
3 Resources of rooming or staffing can only be provided at the expense of other areas of the school and this is not felt to be desirable. The Deputy is in a position to 'cost' the proposal exactly and to demonstrate the likely outcomes.

Much clarification of targets can be undertaken with the Deputy to whom the middle manager reports. It allows for exploration of ideas before firm commitment, and helps to present a case for additional resources where required. Inevitably there will be occasions where a target is strongly supported or opposed by the Deputy Head prior to obtaining the Head's agreement. This is usually because further factors not previously considered have come to light. For this reason, target-setting should be tackled in two phases:

1 Initial planning and discussion with the Deputy Head at a series of meetings with the individual or several members of staff involved.
2 A final meeting with the Head (who has been briefed by the Deputy) with the pastoral or curriculum middle manager, in the presence of the Deputy, at which targets will be set finally if possible.

Target-setting is the logical outcome of evaluation and appraisal. It should be shared with the widest possible range of participants, but the approach outlined here indicates stages by which the Deputy Head can ensure that the process does take place and the energy is not dissipated through lack of a framework to make sure that things happen.

## Living with ambiguity

In Chapter 3, the need for a Deputy Head to be ready to exploit creative contradiction virtually as a condition of appointment was pointed out. Some writers have suggested that the Deputy's work is constantly plagued by uncertainty. Dunham (1984), for instance, divides pressures on Deputy Heads into three main groups:

1 A wide range of responsibilities.
2 Role conflict.
3 Difficult relationships with Head, staff, pupils and parents. (p. 69)

Examples are then given of Deputies trying to reconcile a major teaching commitment with a large number of unpredictable crises, the demands of staff, and a typical situation in which 'the role of the Deputy Head is undefined in a school and role boundaries are unclear between members of the senior management team or between them and middle management'. Dunham (*op.cit*, p. 72). The one characteristic of the Deputy's role in this view is *ambiguity*.

Yet a response to this problem in the form of a rigid job description is to remove ambiguity on paper, but to leave the habits of staff unchanged. Where role conflict is created by the Head's apparent inability to delegate clearly, the Deputy is only experiencing some of the problems of Headship itself. One is that Heads are accountable to the governors alone for the conduct of the school. A tendency of all staff to bring problems to the Head personally unless firmly directed down a line of delegation – and the belief on the part of members of the public, parents, sales people and others that one person is constantly available to deal with all their needs and problems – means that the willingness to deal with a large and varied number of fragmented human contacts is a requirement for at least part of each day.

Ambiguity may create constricting circumstances in which an excess of petty tasks makes working life intolerable. On the other hand, it can be exploited by the Deputy in a way not open to the Head, because the Deputy is not finally accountable for actions or statements to quite the same extent. One way to operate is to become involved in the support of a particular subject area or pastoral initiative through assisting in the writing of a new syllabus or preparation of classroom materials. Discussion of the aims of the material, and learning processes involved, can be supplemented by the informal inspection of written work produced, visiting classrooms to see the material in use and other active involvement. Here, the Deputy is deliberately breaking the artificial boundaries which restrict the role to administration and is becoming involved in fostering a learning initiative. This puts the Deputy in a position of contributing and giving. It is particularly important that an opportunity for such interaction is made from time to time, otherwise the individual is put in a position of appearing to take and dictate excessively – as in the case of the person organising cover for staff absence in a school where the absence rate is high.

Ambiguity of function, however, allows for the setting of priorities, and the very same forces that can lead to work 'overload' may be harnessed to order what is done, and ensure that the most important tasks are accomplished efficiently. If it is not possible to refuse the trivial and unnecessary without causing offence, then it is at least not necessary to let them dominate the working day to the detriment of more pressing professional functions.

Another way of using ambiguity to advantage is to work through the formal structures of negotiation and staff consultation. These should complement and support other staff procedures as well as the work of the other Deputies and Head. For example, the Deputy is the right person to set up study groups or working parties to investigate and report back to the Head or staff meeting on their findings. Such working parties can take two forms. One is that of a standing group in existence to discuss and make recommendations upon permanent aspects of the running of the school, such as the pastoral system. The other is a group with a limited life, set up to report upon a particular issue of concern or interest, say parental communication. A working party could examine the effect of a national initiative upon the school, such as the provisions of an Education Act. The importance of these groups in school management is that they allow the Deputy to work directly with a range of staff who can be selected to represent a variety of ages and interests. It gives the management team a more effective insight into how staff are thinking than sporadic contributions to a full staff meeting, and improves the quality of decision-making through fuller consultation. It ensures additionally that staff are meeting and consulting in groups other than those rigidly associated with the school's formal management structure, such as tutor team meetings with a house head or departmental meetings with a subject head.

As a background to this form of operation around the school, the Deputy should have the resources to maintain a small professional library of current books on education, as well as to store and file copies of syllabuses, LEA circulars, information about courses and publications by HMI and DES. A regular contact with supportive advisers within the LEA is also a useful source of advice, materials and guidance.

We have seen in this section that the Deputy is faced with a stark decision to make when confronting the problem of ambiguity. Although institutional habits and constraints may determine the scope for action, the choice is very often a personal one, depending upon the ability to size up a situation, to identify key components of the school's culture and, if necessary, to take risks. A knowledge of the basic course of action available can help the individual to take an objective view of a subjective role.

Griffith (1966) identified three broad styles of approach which characterised the involvement of central government departments with their local counterparts. They apply usefully to distinguish the ways in which Deputies react to their schools. The categories of response were:

1 Laissez-faire.
2 Regulatory.
3 Promotional.

The *laissez-faire* reaction of the Deputy has been shown earlier in this chapter as a coping strategy when dealing with an extreme confusion of boundaries, responsibilities, and innovations. At times, it is the only response in a school where an ineffective Head is matched by a vigorous middle management operation. The school could thrive in some respects. Innovations and developments often start successfully, but lack 'follow through'. The *regulatory* approach serves best where power is firmly delegated, and there is a requirement placed upon the Deputy to 'police' the use of rooms, monitor finance and orders for stock carefully, and make detailed inquiries into the cause of staff absence, etc. In this atmosphere there is a danger that, if carried to excess, there is less emphasis upon responding to changing circumstances and necessary innovation.

The *promotional* style allows a clear mandate for a creative approach within guidelines which have been agreed by the Head in consultation with other Deputies. It emphasises the responsibilities and authority of other staff, especially the middle managers, but avoids the dogmatism and restrictiveness of hierarchical line management views of schools. It also requires the perception to recognise development and change in micropolitical groupings within the staff, and an understanding of group dynamics, if effectiveness is to be achieved. The way in which these processes involve the Deputy Head will be dealt with next.

## Interest groups

The allegiance of individuals to particular interest groups affects their reactions. Job descriptions and staff handbooks showing the 'chain of command' within a school reveal little of the reality lying behind day-to-day decision-making. For example, it is hardly the intention of such documents to analyse the processes which take place when an outspoken head of a 'practical' subject department who is also the Health and Safety representative of the largest union in the school is trying to refuse to take more than twenty pupils in a fourth-year set, despite having had twenty-two in one set the previous year. In this case, there is clearly much more negotiation to be done, though not without reckoning on the influence fellow union and departmental members will have, or without appreciating the dangers for either person in apparently 'losing face' if conflict becomes over-intense.

The influence of group beliefs and reactions mean that the Deputy is often dealing with fluid opinions and alliances, and represents a part of management which is, in effect, a moving target for the reactions of staff. The political model of management which Bush (1986, *op.cit.*) characterises as assuming that 'policy and decisions emerge through a process of negotiation and bargaining', provides a way of interpreting staff behaviour in school which may otherwise be dismissed as obstructiveness. The concluding sentence of Bush's definition has an even stronger message for the Deputy Head:

> Conflict is viewed as a natural phenomenon and power accrues to dominant coalitions rather than being the preserve of formal leaders. (p. 68)

To ignore conflict or to assume that it does not exist is to proceed in wilful ignorance of the real differences between staff. For example, philosophies over the grouping of pupils by ability may be based upon deeply held social and political beliefs as well as the fact that considerable resources of time have been put into making a particular scheme work in a subject department. An appraisal drawing attention to some shortcomings in a scheme of work might be seen as questioning its fundamental principles. A change in position of a subject on fourth-year options can be taken as a judgement of its lack of suitability for a full range of pupils when the departmental head is adamant that, despite national curriculum guidelines, the subject should be considered as a 'core' experience for all pupils. Deputies should aim to develop a deep and sympathetic understanding of the beliefs of subject or pastoral heads within the school. They should also seek out other opinion leaders who do not necessarily occupy formal positions, but whose virtues of intellect, ability to articulate, subversive sense of humour, or occupation of positions of importance outside the school, give them recognition. Staff who are Justices of the Peace, union officials or important in a local religious or ethnic community, have considerable influence. Cultivation of such contacts gives early warning of impending developments, or of likely reaction within and beyond the school boundaries to proposed change.

Deputies occupy a pivotal point of group interest and conflict when they have any degree of control over the distribution of resources. Timetabling allows control over staff and room allocation, but, even here, custom and practice may be a strong factor in ensuring that certain departments get their way to the detriment of others. If this happens, detailed curriculum analysis to illustrate pupil-teacher ratios in different departments for each age group in the school is a valuable and politically sensitive piece of information to have available for use at the right time. (It is not unknown, given a Head who takes no interest in the distribution of the important resources of staffing between departments, for information to be 'leaked' about differential staffing levels to prepare the ground for a more rational distribution of staff between departments.)

Other sources of power for the Deputy include: access to expertise from the local training institution as a result of links forged through receiving teaching practice students; detailed knowledge of aspects of the school curriculum; and the interests and qualifications of teachers across the school, which enable the arangement of links between staff with common interests. Knowledge of developments in other schools allow for this process to be extended by arranging visits for staff to other institutions, using contacts gained through a Deputy Head's support group of the sort described in Chapter 3.

The next stage of assessing the significance of the influence interest groups have is to watch for key events which trigger the group reactions that determine the meanings people attach to management in school. (After these, almost everyone requires a response from the Deputy Head – often to ameliorate conflict without involving the Head.) The way in which events take their course will vary from school to school. Here are two basic situations:

1 As a result of failing to receive an expected promotion, an individual is proving unco-operative with a newly appointed departmental head. Information is unforthcoming, comments made at departmental meetings are in danger of being an embarrassment to others present, and the quality of classroom work has deteriorated in a previously reliable teacher. This is causing a strain within the department. If no remedial action is taken, then the course of events will be destructive

both of departmental development potential, and for the personal and professional well-being of the dissatisfied individual.

Here, a Deputy can be used to mediate by undertaking an individual counselling session with the member of staff. The session will give an opportunity for an expression of the individual's career frustration and how best to regain a positive approach to the future. It might include arranging for an extension of experience within the school to give a greater chance of future promotion within or beyond the institution. For example, a second in a department, experienced in keeping stock records and registering examination entries, could broaden experience by undertaking home visits with a pastoral head, gaining first-hand knowledge of the pastoral system at work. If the person was unsuccessful simply due to lack of experience compared with the successful candidate, then visits to other schools might be arranged, possibly with the new head of department, with a view to reporting back on particular practices or innovations.

2 A weak head of department is causing dissatisfaction within a departmental team. It is difficult for the Head to take up specific complaints formally at this stage, as they may form the basis of a more serious course of action in the future if improvement is found not to be possible. Furthermore, the individual's personal problems at home are believed to be associated with the deterioration in performance, and it is hoped that time will mean that they are resolved in one way or another. The Deputy is asked to investigate further and see what can be done. It is decided to approach the problem in two ways. Firstly the Deputy will continue a series of one-to-one conversations with the individual to see if the school can help. It might only be to arrange for a series of days to be taken as leave of absence to be designated 'compassionate leave', but this is a practical way of expressing sympathy and volunteering support. Secondly, the problems being experienced in the department are to be broached tactfully, but directly, to see if the head of department perceives them in the same way as do other members of the department. This is to risk an adverse or defensive reaction, but is felt to offer some hope of success in a situation (which must be rectified for the sake of pupils anyway). If this approach is successful, then courses of remedial action can be undertaken. The Deputy can also take action by:

a)  Making sure that the head of department and its members are thanked for any work leading to improved performance of pupils or staff.

b)  Giving support of resources from a contingency fund where appropriate. (This might include re-equipping a part of the department.)

c)  Ensuring that Deputy Head interest is not too intrusive, or given in such a way that it lessens the authority of the head of department, who must be allowed to rebuild credibility with the departmental team.

In both cases, the Deputy has dealt with a key source of destructive tension within a group. The Head may well have been informed of each stage of development, and used the Deputy as a way of avoiding involvement at too early a stage. Successful resolution of the two situations has depended upon:

  1 The Deputy Head's personal standing and skill in staff counselling, and
  2 The availability of some reserve of funds to time to be used at the Deputy Head's discretion.

Having established that interest groups will behave according to their own dynamics, it becomes part of the Deputy Head's job to develop the skills of entry, negotiation and mediation with them. The cultivation of a personal style, and growth of ability to work with groups, which creates an autonomous contribution to school management without in any way diminishing the authority of the Head, is the mark of a skilled Deputy.

# Personal style

If the business of working with groups and individuals around the school is an essential part of the Deputy Head's role in management, no success can be achieved unless the individual is liked and acceptable to staff. This does not mean striving for popularity at any cost, but it does imply that the Deputy Head role involves relationships with a very wide range of staff. If they are warm and cordial, then an atmosphere will be established in which the more difficult occasions – asking someone to improve their classroom performance with a problem child, for example – can be handled without rancour.

Deputies need to recognise that their role is defined partly by staff expectations based upon the folklore of particular staffrooms, by their predecessors, and by the experience of Deputy Heads which individual members of staff had in their own schooldays. This is particularly the case when young teachers or students in teaching practice need support and it is necessary to clarify with them whether a situation is best resolved by a Deputy's input, or by a changed approach on their part.

Many staff demand instant decisions or expect immediate support in dealing with a situation which they could best handle themselves, possessing full relevant background information on a matter. It is important not to be pushed into a decision or to hurry in a crisis. A deferral of a decision is a decision in itself and this may have to be emphasised. It applies especially when dealing with pupil behavioural problems where pressure is being exerted on the Deputy to persuade the child's parents to request a transfer to another school. The child's, and parents', interests are to be considered, and other possibilities such as internal reallocation within the school might have to be looked at first. This takes time, and deferral here would not constitute indecision or weakness. A failure to follow through a problem, or to review the outcomes of a decision after a trial period, would.

One of the quickest ways for a new Deputy to establish successful relationships with staff, or for an experienced Deputy to ensure that proper contact is being maintained, is to cultivate the habit of being *visible*. This is achieved by deciding at which points in the day it is possible to be seen by as many staff as possible around the school. The periods before and after school sessions as well as during lesson changeovers are most useful. In some schools, the Head and all Deputies regularly make it their business to be in the staffroom at certain times of day so that they can be approached easily by staff about concerns as they arise.

It is at times of maximum visibility that good Deputies are able to demonstrate, through their own habits and attitudes, the expectations that the school has about staff-pupil relationships. A school goal 'to establish standards of courtesy and respect for others at all times' is of little meaning unless movement around the school is orderly. It means more if the Deputy Head opens the door for a pupil carrying a pile of books and is seen to be being courteous than if general exhortations are made to this effect in assemblies. This is also a time to encourage dawdling pupils to get to lessons punctually, to be seen by staff to be doing it, and to keep one's ears open. Many a planned fight between pupils after school has been averted by the surreptitious gathering of overheard information and the judicious placing of senior staff in the area when the incident is expected.

Visibility also allows for informal comments to be passed on which provide valuable impressionistic information about staff reactions of importance, for instance to the way in which pupils are settling down at the start of a new term; to the behaviour of a new child which the school has taken in after expulsion from a neighbouring school, or to the fact that the heating is failing to work in a particular room in cold weather.

One of the ways in which the Deputy's informal contribution to management is at its most effective, though most difficult to measure, is in the giving of praise, congratulations and thanks to staff. At times this is a vital aspect of normal courtesy, particularly if a member of staff has organised an event bringing prestige to the school, such as taking the school band to perform at a local festival. The fact that the Deputy has thanked the member of staff personally is helpful if the Head has forgotten under the pressure of work. Even being thanked twice shows that the appreciation of the person's work is widespread! Staff feel supported where their contribution is recognised. Staffrooms become unhappy and demoralised places where significant individuals or groups feel that their contributions are taken for granted or undervalued. The Deputy, as a representative of senior management, should be untiring in efforts to make staff feel that their work is valued. Everyday informal conversation supplements and lends commonplace reality to the more formal processes of evaluation which take place elsewhere.

The opportunity should also be taken to pass on favourable pupil comments about a particular lesson, subject or teacher. Of course, this should never be done with unfavourable comments which may have been overheard, but the positive response should be celebrated. It may also be an opportunity to discuss the work of a particular group of pupils who are showing exceptional progress, interest or enthusiasm, and to negotiate entry into their work, by seeing examples of their achievement in exercise books or visiting a classroom to see a display of work, and pass on encouragement and recognition to the pupils themselves in the teacher's presence.

In schools where this sort of interchange happens and Deputy Heads are seen to be actively involved in encouraging good classroom practice by teacher and pupil alike, there is less likely to be a gulf which exists in many institutions between 'senior management' and 'staff'.

The impression a Deputy makes on people can be improved if an open-door style of working is established within the office. The closed office door is the biggest barrier to communication for a newly arrived member of staff. For the experienced practitioner it can even have the opposite effect of encouraging unwanted non-verbal communication in the form of 'bursting in' or as a handy instrument to slam! It is possible to confirm the importance of whoever comes through the open door by always finding time to greet them courteously and positively, and making time to listen. Even when the Deputy is very busy, there should be a provisional hearing of the problem and firm arrangements made to talk through the issues at another time to be arranged as soon as is mutually convenient.

It is necessary to ensure that the Deputy does not allow her- or himself to be pushed into making sudden commitments. The art of listening should aim both to make people feel that their contribution is important, and also to solve problems. Many people take small-scale problems to a Deputy which they either would not take to the Head, or have felt should be resolved by their departmental or pastoral head but were not. However, many people faced with a problem are aware of possible solutions which they can find themselves, but still seek reassurance. Good listeners use the time to distil essential 'issues from what they are being told, and to feed these back to the talker in the form of potential courses of action from which a choice can be made.

Good listening is part of the Deputy Head's skill in that it has potential to:

1 Stop problems becoming magnified and having to be dealt with by the Head when they could have been resolved at an earlier stage.
2 Protect middle managers from being left with unsolved problems within their area without support from the relevant Deputy.

The greatest achievement in being a good listener is to allow someone with a problem to offer their own solution without being aware of it, or to be given a solution and go away believing that they found it themselves.

Inevitably, humour has a powerful influence on the atmosphere for personal interaction being dealt with here. It is, perhaps, the most individual element of personal style, but its importance should not be overlooked or underestimated. Woods (1979) gave an account of 'the Meaning of Staffroom Humour' with delightful examples of the way in which staff confirmed their solidarity and used it as a coping mechanism to adjust to the alienating effects of school life.

If Deputy Heads can understand its importance for other staff, and to accept that any sign of pomposity, insensitivity in the operation of bureaucratic rituals, or occasional inefficiency is bound to be a target for staff humour, then they are in a better position to share and exchange feelings and reactions with them. The Deputy's sense of humour should never be outrageous or in any way hurtful to staff or pupils. As long as it is there, it will serve to prevent barriers of distance or excessive formality arising.

# Conclusion

We have seen that the management of people's work within the school is a very important part of the Deputy Head's job. At the same time, this process is subject to more uncertainty for the Deputy than for any other level of management in the school, mainly as a result of role ambiguity. There are, however, positive ways to find solutions to the problem. They are based upon recognising the need for structured negotiation to establish the job requirements of major middle management post-holders within the school to and monitor their effectiveness. The Deputy must then undertake target-setting for the relevant pastoral or curriculum areas, sharing this work with the Head as necessary.

Without a philosophy which determines belief in how much autonomy staff may have in managing their own work, the Deputy Head will lack a firm approach to dealing with the micropolitical dimension of the school as expressed by the reactions and movements of various interest groups. The skills of negotiation are essentially political in nature (even though they could be dismissed altogether by those who define school management in purely hierarchical, bureaucratic, structural terms). Nevertheless, the development of an awareness that 'unofficial' processes are an important aspect of staff relationships will assist individual Deputies greatly in coping with and exploiting the ambiguous nature of their role.

# 5 Senior management teams

## Nature of the team

Writers on school management devote much space to the role of the Head (Peters 1976), but little to the nature and development of senior management teams. Ignoring the level of Deputy Headship, literature has concentrated upon middle management in its various forms (Marland and Hill 1981). Though not given credit for it, the Deputy is particularly concerned to relate middle management's actions to whole-school policy. Previous chapters have dealt with the Deputy Head's responsibility to lead and support departmental and pastoral heads. This chapter now deals with the point at which Headship and Deputy Headship meet together – formally and informally. Most teachers in secondary schools are aware of the work of a 'senior management team', consisting of Head and Deputies. The mere use of the term 'team' may not mean that there is one, although a team approach is the strongest way to organise management. Other terms reflect varying philosophies of management, including 'top four', 'the executive', 'administration team', and 'management group'. (Informal terms beloved of staffroom folklore are even more varied, if not so complimentary!) There is a lack of research into how senior management teams compare or contrast in different schools, but such systematic evidence as exists suggests that their nature varies greatly according to the style of Headship in operation, as we shall see. A fuller understanding of Deputy Headship can be reached through examining the operation of senior management teams, and the Deputy's contribution to them.

As described in Chapter 1, the nature of Headship has changed in most schools beyond all recognition. One of the best descriptions of its transformation is the account subtitled *The Headmaster tradition: from autocrat to chief executive* (Morgan, Hall and Mackay, op.cit. 1983). This traces the changes in style of Headship, and in the expectations placed upon the role as schools have expanded and diversified in their functions. A later publication by the same writers (Morgan, Hall and Mackay, 1986) gives details of senior management structures operated by four of the Headteachers whose work was observed. They may be summarised as follows:

### School 1.

Head, First and Second Deputies, Second Master, Director of Studies.

### School 2

Head, Senior Deputy Head, Second Deputy Head, Senior Mistress.

### School 3

Head, Senior Deputy Head, two Second Deputy Heads, three Heads of lower schools.

### School 4

Head, three Deputy Heads, three assistant heads of section, Director of Studies, Pastoral Co-ordinator.

Note: Since 1987, the titles Second Master and Senior Mistress are no longer used for official salary purposes.

The same account shows Heads holding management meetings at differing frequencies. They also varied in the extent to which they met with one, some, or all of their Deputies. The senior team in School 1 met daily on a planned basis. In addition there was considerable informal interchange, with Deputy Heads as well as other staff having frequent access to the Head's office. School 2 represents an extreme contrast to this, with the Head meeting the Senior Deputy for about half an hour each morning, but meeting the Second Deputy and Senior Mistress 'on average, less than once a day'. In other words, Deputies find themselves in teams with a rather arbitrary degree of formality or informality in the way business is conducted. They may also discover that different fellow Deputies work in varying degrees of closeness with the Head.

In a case study of her experiences as a newly appointed Head, Lloyd (1986) describes some early stages in team-building. She draws attention to the problems which existed both for and between Deputies prior to her arrival; problems which are fairly common in schools where the Head has neglected the development of a team approach to management:

> Our meetings were conducted in the only way possible for me. I behaved as myself, confided in them, asked for their help and advice, listened carefully to their suggestions and criticisms, received feedback and relied

on their reminders and creative contributions to problem solving and decision-making. In addition to this atmosphere being ideal for me, I believe it is excellent for staff development, for headship training. The previous Head had never met with them in a trio, had consulted only with the male Deputy and passed on orders and criticisms to the female Senior Deputy who was permitted no curricular contribution at all. Inevitably, the Deputies' relationship had been mutually wary with little trust allowed to develop. Despite the increased honesty of participation, for I was transparent in these encounters, there was an undercurrent of distrust between them and each sought private meetings with me. (p. 41).

In this example, the previous Head's autocratic style had prevented any form of team developing, with unfortunate effects upon the attitude of the Deputies to each other. Changing to a more open style of leadership, the Head placed a high priority on establishing co-operation and trust between Deputies, and with herself. She observed later that there was a development from an earlier stage when the Deputies would report unfavourably upon each other to one in which: 'By the second term some of the insecurity and authority dependence had waned'. (p.41) We see here a Head taking seriously the development of the Deputies as a team. This achievement would go some way to securing proper support for her own success as a Head faced with the task of introducing change into a school.

The notion of a 'team' can be a complacent one, emphasising as it does the virtues of trust and co-operation without specifying links between the group's processes and actual decision-making. It is worth turning to traditional management literature to stress the importance of a balance between individual responsibility and team contribution. Drucker's (1970) comment on the difference between teams and committees may be a little extreme if applied rigidly to school management, but it does help to show how Lloyd's (*op.cit.*) style of work with the Deputies as a group takes place simultaneously with firm individual contribution:

> The first requirement is that it be a 'team' rather than a 'committee'. There should be no collective responsibility. Each member should have assigned to him the areas in which he makes final decisions and for which he is responsible. Deliberation should be joint; decision single. (p. 214)

In practice, the expectations placed upon Heads do not allow the total delegation of areas of decision-making to the Deputy (as demonstrated in Chapter 2), but team effectiveness relies upon the responsibility undertaken by each of its members. A school's senior management team is always constituted *primarily* of the

Head and Deputies, sometimes with the addition of other key staff holding associated responsibilities. It follows that, far from being passively subject to the leadership of the Head, the Deputy should be fully aware of and involved in functions of the management team, of the dynamics of the group, and the means by which it achieves effectiveness. An active, creative contribution is at the same time more supportive than a dependent one, assisting the Head to resist the strains placed upon that office.

# Functions in a school management team

The basic functions of the management team are the same as the basic functions of management itself. In traditional management theory there are four (Hunt, *op.cit.*):

- planning
- organising
- directing
- controlling

In a school, the Deputy will be both sharing these functions and directly exercising them. They range over the need to accomplish long-term and short-term goals, as well as focusing the efforts of individuals upon the team's essential tasks. For example, fourth-year option timetables cannot be constructed without a detailed knowledge of staff likely to be available, and the extent to which this area of the timetable can be given priority over and above other staffing needs, such as the sixth form or provision of administration time for departmental heads. In addition, long-term decisions have to be taken on the basis of predicting existing trends. One instance is the dropping of a second modern language given the experience of low pupil take-up and problems in recruiting qualified staff. This sort of planning is necessary before the work itself – who teaches what and where – can be organised.

A vital part of *planning* rests upon having available the necessary data about a school. Without it, alternative plans and strategies cannot be considered. Basic data includes:

1 Curriculum analysis in diagrammatic form.
2 Staff curriculum deployment analysis.
3 List of all teaching staff; posts of responsibility held.
4 Room list with room usage analysis.

An example of point 2 is given in Chapter 6 and examples of the others in 'Basic timetable data' (see Appendix 4).

In many senior management teams, the use of such data is restricted to the Head and timetabling Deputy. Copies of the analyses should be circulated, read and understood by all members of the team, rather than just these two on their own.

Planning also takes into account knowledge of a school's neighbourhood, of what people are saying about it in local shops and pubs, as well as opinions of the school held by local authority advisers, officers and elected representatives. These are all best gathered by a team who will share perceptions and estimate the likely impact of future changes. This is especially important when managing the effects of falling or rising rolls, of introducing or deleting particular subjects from the timetable, and in identifying which parts of the school need to be run more efficiently.

There are two very different aspects of planning here: the detailed objective data on the one hand, and the astute insights into moods, opinions, shifts in power and intangible realities of the school's environment on the other. Without good Deputies to assist with these two broad requirements of team management, Heads are left with the impossible task of constantly gathering and collating data, and making controversial judgements without the opportunity to share with and test them against the perceptions of fellow members of a non-partisan management team.

Good planning is best tackled like this on a shared basis. The *organising* of practical teaching, induction and guidance of staff, and the training of middle management in how to build up the strengths of individuals in departmental or pastoral teams, comes most effectively from Deputies who make single areas their responsibility and are accountable for their efforts to the rest of the senior team.

*Directing* is a necessary, if pejorative-sounding, term to describe the implementation of detailed policies. To some, the term means 'dictating'. It does not, however, imply that people have not participated in making a decision, although it may imply that a decision has been made infavour of a particular viewpoint and against another. The Deputy in the management team has opportunities to raise matters of contention in advance, in order to make sure that alternatives have been fully considered. This ensures support when difficult timetabling decisions are being taken or when a change of duties is being arranged within the pastoral team. It is important at such times that the whole team is informed and made fully aware of the considerations involved. Without this, individual Deputies may find themselves 'buttonholed' or manipulated by staff who (intentionally or not) end up playing off one member of the senior management team against another.

Finally, the *controlling* function of the senior management team relies ultimately upon the authority of the Head. However, given a degree of unity of purpose established through the support, understanding and mutual intention built up in a good team, staff accept and understand that Deputies are working within the authority of the team, fully shared by the Head and other Deputies, rather than as individuals. (This is not always the case, as we shall see later in this chapter.)

## Contribution and the Deputy

The good Deputy understands and makes a conscious input to each of the team's explicit structural functions outlined above. For this to come about it is necessary for the Head to identify the particular strengths of each Deputy and to seek ways of building upon them.

The foundation of an effective team rests upon individual willingness to focus upon *contribution*. Drucker (*op.cit.*) explains that the effective executive concentrates upon contribution to the performance of the entire organisation, rather than on narrow specialist skills or a particular department. This means that effective Deputies contribute suggestions and data which take into account the effects of proposals and solutions to problems as they affect the whole school, not just the pastoral system, a particular age group or other single aspect of the school for which they are responsible. Contribution also involves willingness, in the right place, to lead particular innovations while they are being implemented on a trial basis and to become personally involved in organisational changes. Timetabling oneself in to take a class within a new programme – for example, of library-based skills, or computer-assisted learning – is a way to monitor activities for the senior management team, as well as to emphasise team support for staff who may be involved at a particularly testing time. Even a comparatively small change, such as an alteration in arrangements to supervise the school at the end of the school day, should involve one or more of the Deputies in its operation for the first week at a minimum. In this way, staff see that the team is active and its members are prepared to ensure *in person* that plans made on paper are working out in practice. An extension of this approach is to attach a Deputy to a particular departmental or pastoral team to assist during a time of particular difficulty, such as the prolonged absence of a head of department or second in department.

As each member of the team focuses upon contribution, it is important to recognise the different types of input made as a result of personality, especially when there is nothing to distinguish between the strengths of personal commitment offered by individuals.

Belbin (1981) believed that the ideal team should contain a mix of personalities fulfilling different types of roles within the group. He suggested there were eight types, summarised below. In parenthesis are examples of how individual Heads and Deputy Heads fall into the categories:

1 The *company worker* – is hard-working, self-disciplined, with sound organisational skills. (Having a good knowledge of the school and its customs, this Deputy works hard at fitting staff and pupils into traditional patterns of curriculum, timetable, behaviour, etc, and implicitly regards predictability as very important.)

2 The *chairperson* – has an even temperament and is very committed to basic objectives. (The Head with a team of intellectually able and creative Deputies who can fulfil this role well, will ensure that innovations and ideas are 'solid' and well-executed. In return, the school will have a sense of direction and purpose.)

3 The *shaper* – challenges conservatism and complacency in the group and, while possessed of nervous energy, may sometimes be impatient. (This ambitious Deputy may be propounding new schemes for developing links with industry, redefining use of a whole suite of classrooms previously thought to belong to one particular department, or eagerly advocating the restructuring of the pastoral system from a horizontal to a vertical grouping arrangement within a few weeks ready for the start of the next school year! Even if not all of the proposals are carried through, the process of re-examining basic objectives is valuable to the group. It may be necessary to dissuade the individual from taking on too much.)

4 The *plant* – is the outstandingly intellectually gifted member of the group: imaginative, knowledgeable, but sometimes impractical. (This Deputy has excellent, if a little generalised ideas about what teaching and learning could be like provided all teachers were utterly inspired with their work, and willing to improvise highly individualised learning programmes for every single pupil they teach, as well as being prepared to work for twenty-five hours in every day!)

5 The *resource investigator* – is energetic, extrovert, full of enthusiasm. (This outward-going Deputy is ideal for establishing contact with advisers, opposite numbers in other schools, middle managers in friendly local industries, and tapping resources of help from parents and other parts of the community. Such individuals sometimes become bored easily and need a mixture of new tasks and frank self-appraisal to maintain full motivation.)

6 The *monitor-evaluator* – is discreet, sober in judgement and even dull. (Here is the perfect foil and balance to some of the less well-thought-out ideas of the plant and the resource investigator.)

7 The *team worker* – is milder than the others, responsive to group and individual feelings, tending to see the 'middle way', sometimes to

the point of indecisiveness in a crisis. (This Deputy helps the team avoid over-reaction and hasty decision-making. Such an approach has its use when two other people in the team have strongly opposed basic beliefs which come to the fore in a particular discussion. The extent to which competition should be promoted in the classroom is an example of the sort of topic which can arouse deeply held antagonisms.)

8 The *complete finisher* – is extremely conscientious; always tries to perform a task perfectly, but tends to worry too much about trivialities. (This Deputy can safely be entrusted with the parts of sensitive administration which require a painstaking approach, but may sometimes become over-anxious, and needs to be taken aside occasionally and quietly helped to get things into perspective.)

In practice, the categories are over-simplified; in real life individuals play different roles at different times, according to their interests and the type of business under discussion. It has to be acknowledged that senior management teams in large schools are often important arenas of debate within the school, subject to Cabinet-style internal tensions. While the Head's role has the power of a figurehead, like that of a Prime Minister (without the inherent instability of needing to obtain the support of an electorate), the Deputy Head at work shares a number of features in common with the role of Cabinet Minister. This takes us beyond the purely managerial aspects of how the senior management team works and into a mixture of its social and micropolitical dynamics. For this reason we must examine the work of the Deputy Head as a 'Cabinet member' in more depth.

Comparisons with a Cabinet help to illuminate those aspects of a senior management team which are concerned with the sharing of power between a small number of individuals, each one of whom is, by virtue of position, highly committed to the school, yet holding detailed responsibility as a Deputy Head. The very intensity of feeling and desire to ensure that the school is running well, creates tensions between people who care alike, have different perceptions of priorities, but know at the same time they must work together for shared ends.

A further analogy is between Head and Prime Minister, as well as Deputy Head team and Cabinet. While it is the case that modern Prime Ministers are described (often perjoratively) as *elected* monarchs, a Head is *appointed* (albeit in former times with almost sovereign powers). Both, however, serve figurehead roles and both work with a team which is supposed to assume overall operational control of affairs. This plurality of role involves the Head in direct dealings with LEA officers, governors and visitors from outside the school to a degree which does not concern the Deputy to the same extent. It is also necessary to arrive at decisions and carry out management processes using the strengths and dynamics of the group. In this, the greatest restraint, as well as the greatest confirmation of power which an individual Deputy holds, lies in the Cabinet term 'collective responsibility'. It implies discretion and confidentiality about sensitive discussions affecting staff, but it must also indicate the willingness to accept responsibility for the outcomes of decisions taken, even when the particular Deputy does not feel fully supportive of the action decided upon. There is no possibility of attempting to win favour from particular groups of staff in the school, either by leaking information or by attempting to disclaim shared responsibility for an unpopular decision. Such pressure will inevitably be brought to bear upon Deputies by members of staff especially in times of change, for example during the course of the first year of a new Head's appointment, but must be resisted.

There are times when Deputies feel compelled to represent drawbacks of a scheme to the Head, especially in cases where the Deputy is more fully aware of the resource implications. It is also the case where the Head wants to foster the career of good, obliging members of staff by giving them more work to do at a time when they are already overburdened with responsibility. Likewise, on occasions when an individual Deputy genuinely believes that staff opinion has reached a point at which the Head and management team should be seen to be taking decisive action, it is a duty to speak out. Such examples can arise when feelings are particularly aroused as a result of a single serious incident with a pupil, or when damage has been caused or vandalism has taken place on site. Here, good Heads are often grateful for the decisive intervention of a committed Deputy, and may well remember that accepting the view of responsible post-holders is not necessarily a weakness in leadership. An example from history reflects this:

> Churchill prodded, cajoled, goaded, upbraided and occasionally tormented the Chiefs of Staff. But if all his powers failed to shift them, he accepted their view. (Gilmour, 1971, p. 208)

Perhaps the same should be said also of the way in which Deputies lead their teams of pastoral or subject heads. The comparison between Cabinet Minister and Deputy Head ends at the point of resignation and dismissal, for all practical purposes. Nevertheless, sincere disagreements can and do occur. Here, an open statement of differing basic beliefs and approaches may do much to sustain the continuing degree of co-operation necessary to work together. While loyalty is vital, it means more than the one-dimensional subservience to the will of one person. It must allow for a full exploration of issues between Deputies in an atmosphere of mutual confidence where problems can be examined in all their complexity, rather than rushing into solutions which the Deputies think the Head wants.

One more analogy between Cabinet and management group is that Heads, like Prime Ministers, are sometimes inclined to set up inner Cabinets, whether formally or informally. Gilmour (*ibid*), gives a number of examples of Prime Ministers who tended to select inner Cabinets from those who agreed with them, rather than those who disagreed! Given the normal maximum of three Deputies, it is better that there is a fair amount of agreement between them in the first place, and that a conscious effort is made by Head and Deputies to listen to dissident voices in the school outside the team. The inner-Cabinet tendency is to be avoided in cases where it starts to act as a filter to make alternative opinions go unheard and unheeded. It is always in danger of being seen as conspiratorial in nature, not just by those excluded, but by staff in general. Worse than that is the 'dynamic duo' syndrome in which a single Deputy or other senior member of staff is regarded as being the confidant of the Head. Whether justified or not, it is a symptom of the breakdown of rational management within a school, as emotion and envy take over from reason. It should always be challenged positively by attempting to ensure that all major issues and decisions are discussed properly at each formal meeting of the senior management team before implementation.

There are special considerations which Deputy Heads bring to the management team unlike those in any other political or commercial management group. They arise from the historical and social nature of the role of Head. This unique position has been underlined by HMI (1977) in their booklet *Ten Good Schools* when they discuss leadership:

> Emphasis is laid on consultation, teamwork and participation, but without exception, the most important single factor in the success of those schools is the quality of leadership of the Head. (p.35)

Their definition of the 'quality of leadership' is somewhat elusive:

> Without exception, the Heads have qualities of imagination and vision, tempered by realism, which have enabled them to sum up not only their present situation but also future attainable goals. They appreciate the need for specific educational aims, both social and intellectual, and have the capacity to communicate these to staff, pupils and parents, to win their assent and to put their own policies into practice. Their sympathetic understanding of staff and pupils, their accessibility, good humour and sense of proportion and their dedication to their task has won them the respect of parents, teachers and taught. They are

conscious of the corruption of power and though ready to take final responsibility they have made power-sharing the keynote of their organisation and administration. Such leadership is crucial for success and these schools are what their Heads and staff have made them. (p. 35)

Although this verges on the platitudinous, it does clearly indicate the gravity of expectations and pressure placed upon Heads. They are bound to feel compelled to ensure that none of the many aspects of the school are failing. In this context, the job of Deputy is to contribute to the more intangible aspects of successful Headship by helping Heads to identify and to build upon their own strengths. They do this not only by acting as communicators with staff, but also by asking the right questions within the management team. At times, it is helpful to check the range of areas of questioning about a proposal or innovation. The quotation above suggests a number of questions which should be asked when the time is appropriate:

1 Have the aims of an innovation been clearly and fully communicated? Should the Deputies be making a combined effort to ensure that this is so?
2 Can a new course realistically offer success to the full range of pupils who will be taking it?
3 Are any groups of staff or individuals unhappy about specific courses of action the team is planning? If so should they be approached quietly by a designated Deputy Head to obtain a fuller knowledge of their point of view?
4 Is the team (with the Head) guilty of corruption of power? e.g. by taking for granted the goodwill and co-operation of a particular group of staff in an innovation which has not been thought through sufficiently?

Headship has always been a lonely job. When questions like these are being answered well, and there is a feeling of achievement or elation by staff, it is as well for the Deputy to inform the Head. We all need our share of good news.

## Meetings and agendas

The size and complexity of the school will determine the number of meetings which are possible or desirable. In some establishments, senior management groups meet daily before school starts for a fifteen-minute review of daily tasks ahead, as well as to allow the Head early warning of issues arising from staff, pupils or the community. It is important that the meeting is brief and that Deputy Head contributions are subject to self-discipline. They should not extend into discussions requiring more time to complete. A longer, weekly meeting of the team is almost certainly essential in a large school. Some Heads use a standing agenda to structure the main meeting. An example of this is given in Appendix 5.

Another way of ensuring efficient working contact is for each Deputy to have a one-to-one weekly meeting with the Head for thirty minutes, in which specific concerns of the individual Deputy can be reviewed. This allows for the exploration of issues which may still be taken up at a meeting of the whole team, but enables the Head to feel aware of a situation, or to seek more information before presenting planned solutions to a problem or placing an issue on the general agenda for the team. Although time constraints may pose problems and one-to-one briefings have to be cancelled when interviews take place or the Head is called away to a meeting, the weekly personal briefing is especially valuable where either the Head or one of the Deputies is new in post.

Other types of meetings include the long-term planning session which takes place over one or more days at a weekend, preferably off the school premises. A teachers' centre provides the right sort of setting: away from the immediate concerns and interruptions of the working week, but with facilities for business-like discussion. This allows for issues to be 'brainstormed', and local authority advisers or other guest speakers to address the group at times when long-term change is being considered for the school, or when there have been a number of personnel changes in the senior team.

Another key to the extent to which Deputies in the group work together lies in the physical positioning of their offices and workspaces around the buildings. One approach is to base a Deputy in each section of a multi-block school, or on each site of a split-site school. The opposite of this is to have Deputies actually sharing an office as an act of deliberate policy, so that they can gain a practical appreciation of each other's work. With this arrangement, it is likely that an interview room will need to be provided where staff or parents can go to speak to an individual Deputy in confidence about personal matters without interruption.

## Phases of growth in management groups: the Deputy's contribution

School senior management groups develop through stages and Deputy Heads develop with them. Changes in membership of the group alter its pattern of growth. A mixture of processes can take place when a new Deputy joins an established group of other Deputies and the Head, or when a new Head joins a group with established Deputies. In both circumstances, one member new to the school should approach its procedures and idiosyncrasies with an open mind. There is much to be learned – even if only to gather the evidence that change is needed! Open minds are also required from established Deputies adjusting to a new Head. Their own habits and assumptions may come under closer scrutiny than they expected. For several months, an experience of healthy uncertainty and self-questioning is a pre-condition to the sound establishment of a new team.

Groups containing a majority of new members may have to go through a growth phase akin to adolescence. They must accommodate a temporary glut of new ideas. People, too, have to pass through a stage of getting to know each other's professional strengths and which assumptions can or cannot be made about their roles in the group. Here, Deputy colleagues should consult each other carefully before proceeding with plans. Never arrange for a colleague to be invited on a course if one's fellow Deputy is unable to arrange cover, for example. New ideas about how to collect timetable data or suggestions concerning a new code of classroom procedures may have worked well in a previous school. In a new school they should not be presented in a raw state but modified for fresh circumstances. A state of maturity is reached in a mangement group when it can accept criticism from within and consider new ideas without feeling threatened by them.

An established group working with a new Head goes through a phase of testing out, possibly attempting rejection, and finally aligning itself, after adjustment, with the new Head's approach to management. Changes to procedure can be difficult to accept for a Deputy with an efficient and established administration system, say of pupil records or substitution for staff absence. Provided the changes are regarded as a new project, and instituted methodically, the Deputy Head should aim both to carry out the change, and to support it on behalf of the Head by explaining its aims to the staff affected. This is always a delicate period if the Head is attempting a great degree of reform. It must be fully understood and communicated to other staff in a manner supportive of the Head if the organisational equilibrium of the school is to be maintained. However, it is at such a time that the senior management group itself is also working to establish its own new balance. In this period of change, the qualities of tolerance, understanding and personal strengths of the Deputy are under their greatest test.

## Deputising

It is a function of the team to provide individuals able to undertake the task of *deputising*. The ability to deputise effectively is only one requirement among many for the Deputy Head, but it is important not to be found lacking in skill and technical knowledge when the time comes for a Head to be absent – in planned or unplanned circumstances. Heads may be absent on business for professional associations, examination board work, or civic duties, as well as for in-service training. Membership of the senior team should prepare all Deputies to be aware of the limits to decisions they may take in the Head's absence, and to gauge those limits according to the length of absence of the Head.

Deputies should be sufficiently briefed to take over in unexpected emergencies or during times when the Head is absent due to illness. Apart from taking staff meetings, or attending governors' meetings, the Deputy should be able to take over routine correspondence, authorise dispatch of references (provided an outline already exists for the individual in question), and generally to retrieve information from the filing system in operation.

In multiple-Deputy schools, as we saw in Chapter 1, it is necessary to designate one Deputy – preferably the longest serving – to deputise in the Head's absence. For longer absences of the Head, say for a term or more, an Acting Head should be appointed and paid as such. It would be unfair on the individual and on the staff to expect someone to deputise for an extended period otherwise.

## When the team does not function properly

In each local authority, advisers and senior officers are generally able to categorise schools according to their effectiveness and overall state of organisational health. They fall into three main categories (not usually identified as such in public):

1 Outstanding schools which achieve a high degree of excellence in fulfilling a range of functions, given their catchment area and resources.
2 Schools which perform competently.
3 Schools which underperform, even when particular features such as catchment area are taken into account, which fail in a number of major functions, and are a cause of serious concern.

It is likely that a Deputy taking up a post in a category 3 school will find that the root of the problem lies with the senior management group. Nevertheless, it may be difficult to locate precise responsibility for the failure. Where uncertainty exists, it should also be remembered that just because procedures are confused and the climate of the team is uncomfortable and frustrating for an individual Deputy, it does not automatically follow that the Head and Deputies are not performing effectively as far as outcomes are concerned. At times frustration may result from a deliberate policy of the Head, but such an approach has at least one strong historical precedent:

> Disordered administration, when intentional, is not without advantages. Roosevelt is said to have avoided laying down clear-cut lines of authority in order to keep decisions in his hands. The resulting quarrels and confusion compelled the various antagonists to come to the White House for the imposition of terms of peace. (Gilmour, *op.cit*, p. 182)

Unfortunately, the smaller size of a secondary school means that the confusion and frustration are then shared by a large proportion of staff. A result of the encouraging of competitiveness between Deputies is that the team's effectiveness in taking a whole-school view of problems is reduced. Deputies compete to promote personal schemes or to seek the Head's support for their own particular field – be it the pastoral system, for example, or the school's community effort. While insecurity may stimulate ambitious Deputies to work hard in the hope of future promotion, it tends to define Deputy Headship as a merely transitory role: an assumption this book contests. On the other hand, if the Head finds the imposition of 'terms of peace' effective, and this style is readily accepted so that an acceptable working atmosphere is assured, then doubts still remain: it is questionable whether 'quarrels and confusion' should ever have occurred in the first place, given the fact that Deputies were being open with each other in providing information. In other words, the situation is likely to have come about through the failure of one or more members of the group to operate efficiently and co-operatively.

Causes of failure in school senior management groups arise either from Deputies' or from the Head's deficiencies. Deputy failure is often the product of one of these four factors:

1 Overload of a single Deputy.
2 Underload of a single Deputy.
3 Inertia or inward-looking tendency of group.
4 Role conflict.

Overloading and underloading of Deputies are symptoms of the same problem: the failure to analyse how significant and time-consuming tasks are distributed. It also arises from changing circumstances which might not have been taken into account when tasks were first allocated. For example, if the LEA's policy on provision of supply teachers changes, increasing the demand for supply cover, without providing additional staff for the purpose, then the Deputy charged with telephoning through the list of available supplies will be spending much more time on that particular job. Deputies may also be overloaded at certain periods of the year. Trying to organise examinations at the same time as monitoring residential experiences in the summer term is an example of an insensitive combination of tasks which would be better shared between two or more Deputies.

Overcoming inertia, or the team's inward-looking nature, is a particular frustration for a new Deputy joining an established group, especially if the school is in obvious need of reform, the role of the Deputy is undervalued, and the newcomer is expected merely to administer the deficient systems already in existence. It is important to establish tactfully whether or not the Head wants new ideas and, if not, the reason for thinking that they are not required. Underlying inertia is sometimes a symptom of deeper insecurity and anxiety, and it is important to recognise its hidden causes.

For example, change in curriculum content, in pupil ability grouping, or in the system of sanctions may be associated generally with 'lower standards'. Even if this is not the case, the way in which parents and the community interpret a change can still give rise to apprehension on the part of the Head. Other long-serving members of the group may have previous uncomfortable experience to justify their negative reactions to an oblivious newcomer.

'Role conflict' has been identified by Dunham (*op.cit.*) as a serious and frequent problem for Deputy Heads. It arises mainly in situations when role boundaries between members of the senior management team, or between them and middle management, are unclear. Dunham (*ibid*) gives an example of a Deputy under stress who believed that the conflict was, in part, deliberately created by the Head, and suggests that Deputies are particularly affected by role conflict when trying to mediate between staff and the Head. Stress created by these experiences, if not managed honestly and thoughtfully, leads to a loss of vitality and enthusiasm in other aspects of the Deputy's contribution to the senior group.

Failure of a Head's performance always has an inescapable effect upon Deputies, either by creating conditions in which it is difficult or impossible for them to do their jobs properly, or in which they feel compelled to undertake the thankless task of 'covering up' and compensating. Before taking positive action, it is necessary to identify the problems which the Head is facing. These could include:

1 Apathy or exhaustion.
2 Excessive complacency, or susceptibility to flattery.
3 Inability to adjust to a rapid turnover of staff, especially at senior and middle management levels.
4 Inability to establish divisions of task between Deputies.

Whatever the problems, good Deputies should always try to recognise a Head's weaknesses, and complement them with their own strengths. For instance, a Head who enjoys contact and socialising with staff, who knows them well as people, and is well-liked at a personal level, but inclined to lack thoroughness in checking administrative detail, may be persuaded to hand over initial drafting and checking of a task like reference writing to a Deputy.

More serious as a problem are cases where Heads are suffering from stress-induced apathy, or have lost interest in a school they intend to leave. This creates a time of uncertainty in which the Deputies' duty is to reassure staff and to react positively to criticisms and suggestions about the school, while trying to put them into order for presentation to the newly appointed Head for consideration. Again, it is a thankless task, as LEA officers and advisers direct their attention to the appointment of the new Head, regardless of the fact that the reactions of Deputies to the appointment, and the way it is made, may have a powerful influence upon staff opinion and help to prepare the way for the arrival of the new Head.

Complacency is often found where a school has been outstandingly successful in the past – be it as a well-publicised, innovatory comprehensive school, or as a respected, traditional, academic institution with a strong local reputation. An exaggerated belief in achievements of the school on the part of the Head leads to any suggestion from a new Deputy for further reform being seen as an implied criticism of the school or its past achievements. Tact on the part of the Deputy is hardly appropriate if staff disaffection is spreading about the lack of development in the school to such an extent that it is affecting their own careers or the achievement of pupils.

Adjustment to a fast turnover of Deputies is a problem for Heads. It requires a rapid and thorough restatement of the aims of the school, and the underlying assumptions made about daily tasks expected of the Deputies, especially if they are external appointments. Good Deputies will have the perceptiveness to induct themselves as far as possible, but they will need time for guidance and briefings which themselves can be used to weld working relationships. Failure to ensure the proper induction and support of a new Deputy leads to the sort of confusion which has further implications across the school. It may be difficult for an outsider, or even a local authority adviser who knows the school well, to determine when a failure to adjust should be attributed to the Head (who may blame the poor appointees themselves), and how far the new Deputies need support and direction additional to that which the Head can reasonably be expected to give. Certainly, if the Head is corrupted by power in some of the ways described above, and has judgement clouded by the effects of flattery and opinions of those seeking preferment, then it will be difficult to exploit the talents of new Deputies and define their roles in a rational way.

Clear divisions of responsibility along the lines explored in Chapter 2, as well as a refusal to allow a single Deputy or any other member of staff to become a particular confidant or unofficial chief ideologue, all help to keep decision-making as an open process, and to avoid the alienation of particular individuals.

## Poor team performance: strategies for Deputies to overcome it

As we have seen above, the causes of poor team performance are varied. Because they involve a limited number of personalities, their interpretation is likely to be rather subjective, involving questions of personal management style and the need to establish a standard of management. However difficult evaluation may be, it is an inescapable responsibility of the Deputy to analyse prevailing circumstances and to take action when they are unsatisfactory. The first response should be to take action of the sort suggested in the following five-point plan. It illustrates a standard management procedure, applied to Deputy Headship:

1 *Define the problem and create new definitions.*
There have been generalised complaints of low staff morale in the school. These are accepted at face value by the Head who repeats them to the Deputies. They seem to be held responsible. A more detailed understanding of staff feeling is required. A new definition of the morale problem could be arrived at by examining specific causes of staff dissatisfaction: if each element is listed and responsibility assigned to individual Deputies for response, then morale will improve as action is seen to be taken. Examples of issues which benefit from such an approach include: establishing easily understood procedures for dealing with acute classroom crisis; the lack of coffee cups in the staffroom; apparent failure by the Head or Deputies to take action over the

behaviour of a persistent staff absentee, or any evidently unresolved problem of discipline with pupils.

2 *Collection and publishing of data.*

The need for availability of basic data has been emphasised earlier in this chapter. Additional data must be gathered to investigate complaints or problems. In a case where, for example, there has been widespread comment about the poor physical state of the classrooms and allegations that the Head and Deputies do not appear to care, the mere act of undertaking a detailed check of the classrooms concerned is a first stage of dispelling ill feeling. Appendix 7 gives an example of a 'request for repairs' form, and a repairs analysis file proforma. With this to hand, it is possible to collate details of the average time taken to respond to a request. Now is the time to be seen by staff to be inspecting the places most urgently in need of attention.

3 *Ask for the acceptance of outside advice.*

Poorly performing teams are often inward-looking and complacent. The suggestion that things are done better elsewhere is a difficult one for them to come to terms with. Bringing in an outsider will probably be the best course of action, although it has to be arranged very tactfully. Organising a visit for a colleague from another school is another way to bring in ideas. The visitor might, for instance, come to meet several members of the pastoral staff. In the course of the day a return visit is arranged for the Deputy Head (pastoral) and Head, to discuss an alternative form of pastoral middle management structure.

A more direct approach is to ask for a local authority adviser to address the senior management group on a theme related to underperformance. This, however, will require a consensus that reform is needed in the first place.

4 *Seek authorisation to take over a complete task independently of present arrangements.*

Team performance suffers when more than one person is constantly trying to take the initiative in order to overcome frustration with the way things are being done. It also suffers in teams where there is personal insecurity and members feel the need to dominate or impress others. Another cause of ineffectiveness is when several people are trying to carry out a task best left to one. An example of this 'too many cooks' tendency is when the Deputy responsible for timetabling has completed the job according to the deadlines previously agreed by the management team. New demands are suddenly made from another Deputy at the end of the summer term to put group tutors onto the tutorial programme teaching their own groups. This leads to chaotic last-minute adjustments and rewriting, with effects of uncertainty and confusion among the subject heads who have spent long hours planning next year's teaching programme around the assumption of given staff teams.

It would be better here to emphasise that one Deputy alone will have responsibility for timetabling and that, after a given date, no major new constraints or changes in structure will be possible.

5 *Find ways to help relieve stress on a fellow Deputy or the Head.*

A team can suffer from problems which seem to be caused by the Head or the actions of one Deputy. Informal intervention can do much to solve the problems by restoring trust and frank communication. In a case where several members of staff are upset by the way a Deputy has handled their request for time out to take a school party abroad, these reactions can be conveyed quietly. It may be that there are reasons for the reaction, of which the staff are unaware. Explanation by an additional Deputy will emphasise the reasons and dispel any impression that the first Deputy was acting as a result of a whim.

In an instance where staff have reacted badly because the Head refused to close the school in exceptionally bad weather, even though neighbouring institutions did close on the same day, the Deputy is likely to be defending the decision to staff. At the same time, there is an obligation to try to overcome the effects of poor communication and to forsee likely points of conflict in order to help the Head overcome them.

Obviously, when things go wrong, the existence of good social contact within the team is as important as the systematic five-point approach. However, there are many instances when informal relationships cannot be relied upon; for example, when one or more of the Deputies is new to the post, or if a member of the group is frequently absent due to illness. When this happens, the duty still remains not to allow underperformance to 'ride' but to take logical and positive steps to improve it.

During times of extreme confusion, the keeping of a detailed private diary (to be kept at home rather than on the school premises) is a helpful aid in analysing events and in continuing to develop personal problem-solving skills. Theoretical solutions can be developed even though there is no opportunity to exercise them in practice. For Deputies preparing for Headship, bad experiences in a senior management team, unfortunate as they are, give a valuable insight into how *not* to manage, and can be used to prepare alternative strategies for use in a later Headship post.

Finally, there are particularly serious cases where the Deputy may have a formal grievance against the Head, after a normal relationship has completely broken down. This should only happen in the most exceptional circumstances, and there are few instances where blame is unlikely to be attached to both parties if even a few of the suggestions contained in this chapter have been followed. In such an eventuality, a Deputy registering a complaint about a Head is invoking the formal grievance procedure of the institution, whereas a Head making a complaint about a Deputy is operating disciplinary procedures. This exceptional course of action should never be taken hastily or lightly. The General

Secretary of one teachers' association recommends that advice should *always* be taken before any action, if necessary by telephone (AMMA, 1984) p. 69.

## Conclusion

In the senior management group, whether it consists of Head and Deputies, or these plus a number of other senior members of staff, the Deputy should focus clearly upon a specific area of contribution. Overlap of responsibility between Head and Deputy and between Deputies themselves is to some extent unavoidable, even desirable, but Deputies can do much to help themselves understand their own strengths in the team and their contribution to it.

By understanding the functions of the team, its internal dynamics, and the duty to be personally supportive and loyal to the Head, Deputies perform a unique function in the management of large schools.

# 6 Seven key tasks

## Timetabling in perspective

The first challenge to any person new to timetabling is that more opinionated nonsense is talked about it than any other single task which falls to the Deputy Head. Some Headteachers and most local authority advisers will never have assumed full operational responsibility for the intricacies and resolution of detail of timetable construction in a large secondary school. Departmental heads vary considerably in the quality of the understanding of whole-school processes that they have derived from involvement in timetabling, although lack of understanding will rarely deter individuals from commenting freely! As a result, gratuitous advice is always available, based upon overheard scraps of wisdom which individuals have picked up, such as: 'Banding will give greater flexibility', or 'You could timetable my subject quite satisfactorily in the mornings; it all depends which other subjects you block first'. The experienced timetabler overcomes this by becoming a teacher of colleagues, pointing out to them the practical consequences of their well-intentioned advice.

In practice, the timetable should be a practical definition of the school's curriculum philosophy, demonstrating the best deployment of people, space and facilities throughout the school day. It follows from this that timetabling should be a whole-year process, directly related to the annual curriculum decision-making chart (see Appendix 2), involving and understood by as many staff as possible. This is in contrast to timetabling as a single, annual event in which not much can be changed because its processes remain a mystery to most staff, including the Head and fellow Deputies. At the same time, however, when effective involvement has been achieved from a wide range of staff, final authority for making inevitable mechanical compromises should rest with the responsible Deputy after consultation with the Head. The right to challenge and delay essential decisions can lead to departmental heads having a detrimental effect upon the efficiency of the whole school, and Heads should treat appeals with discretion when they are made at a late stage in timetable construction.

In the examples of staff criticism given above, it should be made clear that *someone* has to teach third-year pupils last thing on a Thursday and Friday afternoon, and it is generally not possible to timetable 'practical' subjects for the whole school exclusively in the afternoon, leaving the Modern Languages and Mathematics Departments idle at the same time. The problem of self-streaming options cited is in part a matter of policy, and is always greater the larger the proportion of the school week devoted to 'optional' subjects.

Against this background, timetabling is the single task which, alone, often produces the greatest apprehension and feeling of nervous foreboding in a newly appointed Deputy. It presents a probably unique combination of pressures arising from the micropolitics of any school, in which departmental heads feel a need to protect their own areas, however clear their own thinking might be about the whole curriculum in other contexts. The fact that the detailed working through of staffing and rooming is a large logistical task, yields endless potential opportunities for judgements to be challenged or incompetence to be alleged where the school working atmosphere is unsatisfactory for other reasons. At such times, the forces which apparently conspire to prevent the task ever being finished on time seem to be overwhelming.

Faced with these daunting demands, new Deputies should be prepared by undertaking a timetabling course or, failing that, to have studied material such as that by Spencer (1981) in the Open University Management and the School course. It is as well to ignore at this stage the suggestion that every school is different, and that nothing can be taught or learned of common applicability to the timetabler.

A new Deputy arriving in a school where the timetable is in operation should ensure that a full curriculum analysis is available and understood. The number of staff deployed to teach a set number of tutor groups in a particular year for a particular subject should be determined, but other variations should also be noted. Which groups are setted by ability? Which groups take part in a 'circus' arrangement in Art and Design, for instance? If the school and the previous Deputy have been less than well-organised, then the information will have to be gathered by a painstaking analysis of the timetable provided. This assumes that it is running efficiently in the first place, and that the immediate need is not to sort out numerous problems left by one's predecessor.

Staff deployment and curriculum analysis are the best way to get to the bottom of what is going on, as well as to prepare for changes such as alterations in the roll and hence the number of groups in each year, with the commensurate change in staffing allocation which is likely to be imposed. Such an analysis also presents the same information in different configurations for varying purposes. Table 6.1 is an example of a departmental staffing requirement for an 11–16 school with a forty-period week, and an eight-form entry in each year, taught by a department in tutor groups of thirty pupils, except for a fourth- and fifth-year information technology course available to sets selected in the school's options system. No differential arrangements for banding are assumed in this case.

| NAME OF DEPARTMENT: MATHEMATICS | | | |
|---|---|---|---|
| Year | Periods per week | Teaching groups | Teaching period requirement |
| 1 | 5 | 8 | 40 |
| 2 | 5 | 8 | 40 |
| 3 | 5 | 8 | 40 |
| 4<br>4 options | 5<br>3 | 8<br>1 | 40<br>3 |
| 5<br>5 options | 5<br>3 | 8<br>1 | 40<br>3 |
| others: | | | |
| Administration | 3 | | 3 |
| Social Education | 6 | | 6 |
| 2nd subject 'output' | 10 | | 10 |
| | | Total | 225 |

Table 6.1 Departmental Staffing Requirement

Staff deployment analysis is then carried out to determine how an individual's time is distributed across year teaching. This may be done alphabetically for the whole staff, or arranged in hierarchical salary status. Departmental analysis enables quick reference between requirements (as shown in Table 6.1) and staff input, shown in Table 6.2.

| Staff number | Staff code | Name | Responsibility | Full time equivalent | M/F | Periods taught by year | | | | | Total teaching in dept. | Non teaching | Other teaching | Total |
|---|---|---|---|---|---|---|---|---|---|---|---|---|---|---|
| | | | | | | 1 | 2 | 3 | 4 | 5 | | | | |
| 47 | FM | P. Johnson | Faculty Head | 1 | F | 5 | 5 | 5 | 8 | 8 | 31 | 8 | 1 | 40 |
| 2 | DH | A. Crowhurst | School Deputy | 1 | F | — | — | — | 5 | — | 5 | 28 | 7 | 40 |
| 48 | JMK | J. Khan | Junior School Liaison | 1 | M | 10 | 5 | 5 | 5 | 8 | 33 | 5 | 2 | 40 |
| 49 | PMS | P. Smith | — | 0.6pt | M | 5 | 5 | 5 | — | — | 15 | 3 | 6 | 24 |
| 28 | DMH | D. Hughes | — | 1 | M | 10 | 5 | 5 | 8 | 8 | 36 | 4 | — | 40 |

Table 6.2 Staff Input Analysis

The effect of staff leaving can be shown clearly as a period-input shortfall, and with Tables 6.1 and 6.2 it is also possible to calculate the effects of altering the amount of time given to a subject within the week and the saving or increase on the staff requirement generated. Another important reason for gathering such information is that it can be used to show provisionally whether or not a timetable embodying given amounts of time and teaching group sizes for each subject is likely to be feasible. It is vital that this information underpins discussions with the Head about vacancies, and is readjusted in the summer up to the final point at which resignations can be received to take effect for autumn.

The next stage, potentially the most difficult, is to 'block in' teaching groups for the whole school across the week. If, as is the case in many schools, it is possible to deal with half-year groups or even a whole year at a time, then the job of initial blocking is considerably simplified. It is obviously less of a task to timetable and bear in mind the constraints for ten groups consisting of four tutor groups each, totalling 120 periods, than to timetable forty single tutor groups of thirty pupils each. The other advantage is that this can allow departments or faculties a greater degree of autonomy over how staff are deployed within their subject times.

The act of 'blocking' here must be done by one person who is aware of all major constraints, at least for the first stage. In most schools fourth-year option groups are not easily changed and 'roll through' intact into the fifth year. In a school where there are no major changes in curriculum time, numbers on roll and staff allocations, a swap of fourth and fifth year, with years one and two either rolling forward or staying the same, gives a satisfactory 'status quo' starting point from which a new Deputy can produce a timetable outline for the following year. However, there are two general categories of constraint on the timetable which affect this. The first change from year to year and the second are fixed. Year-to-year changes to be considered might be:

1 Links with other institutions such as Further Education colleges, or 'federation' provision for modular curriculum elements, or sixth-form provision.
2 Physical Education use of external facilities such as swimming pools or sports centres.

The second category, of more permanent constraints, is then taken into account:

1 Fourth-year options usually roll through without change.
2 'Practical' areas, such as science laboratories, physical education facilities and CDT areas, are often limited and must be timetabled first.
3 Subjects requiring 'double' or longer combinations of periods must be timetabled before 'singles', even though this may then create further challenges to ingenuity in order to spread single period subjects, say languages and mathematics, across a week.
4 The need to provide certain cross-departmental staffing, such as a social education team of form tutors, may be established as a matter of school policy, although this is bound to be done at a cost to other needs.

Once 'blocking' is completed, 'staffing up' may begin. If staffing for each department has already been calculated and constraints are fully understood by all concerned, then this stage can be undertaken either by heads of department, or by the timetabler. Problems of co-ordination may be encountered at times of staffing reduction and, the smaller the school, the more likely it will be that the staff will have to be used for second or non-specialist subject teaching. These problems are fewer where proper preparation has preceded the timetabling process, and the compromises the timetabler expects to make are readily understood and supported by the Head and fellow Deputies. Whatever happens, the availability of an assistant is always desirable when checking the final timetable as issued, to ensure no duplication of staff in rooms, or staff with teaching groups.

The mechanics of actually writing up and presenting the timetable should be considered at an early stage. If the pencil and rubber system is used, then how will the final timetable be duplicated and distributed, if at all? Will individual staff timetables be copied out by departmental heads, or by the timetabler (a time-consuming task at a period in the school year when a Deputy should also be assisting with other matters such as last-minute appointments, or last-minute adjustments to the timetable itself)?

Spencer (*ibid*) and Johnson (1980) have both discussed the relative merits and demerits of the main wall-display systems on the market. These are most helpful in timetable checking, and are valuable in displaying the timetable as it grows in the course of construction. Their disadvantages are that all the completed workings must still be transferred to paper for distribution, and the pegs and stickers necessary for their operation are easily misplaced. There are several forms in which the timetable may be issued, each one suitable for different purposes:

1 A 'staffing master' showing the timetables of all staff, listed in alphabetical order, with their subjects and rooms for the week.
2 A rooming timetable.
3 Departmental timetables.
4 A year-by-year timetable.

The advent of the microcomputer (functioning here as a data processor, rather than as an instrument to solve timetabling problems) enables these variations to be produced after the data has been typed in once only. It can also be used to check for accidental double-booking of staff or rooms, and can easily print out new editions of the timetable created by changes in staffing during the school year. Again, an assistant is of value for a timetable checked on a board system or initially prepared on paper to be dictated to a keyboard operator and then be re-checked for errors by the computer a second time.

The conclusion of a timetable process is also the starting point for improvements the following year. Spencer (*op.cit.*) suggests fourteen criteria for an objective appraisal of the timetable:

1 Does the timetable represent, in tabular form, the educational philosophy of the school?
2 Are the staffing requests of the heads of department satisfied?
3 Are subjects satisfactorily distributed through the timetable cycle?
4 Are subjects treated fairly by all having a fair distribution of lessons throughout the day?

5 Are specialist rooms and other scarce resources used to the best advantage?

6 Are class timetables balanced and do all classes have a fair share of experienced staff?

7 Is the timetable simply but attractively presented?

8 Have all fixed points been observed?

9 Have all the setting links been observed?

10 Are classes for one subject taken by one teacher? Or, if shared, has this sharing been planned?

11 Has movement been kept to a minimum?

12 Is cover for absent staff feasible?

13 Is the staff non-teaching time reasonably spread?

14 Does the timetabling facilitate curriculum continuity for the following year – and the year after that? (p. 88)


A systematic consideration of each of the criteria allows the timetabler to demonstrate which compromises were made and why. It also indicates the degree of ingenuity, cunning and logical prowess in which the experienced timetabler takes a delight. During the second and subsequent year of timetabling, it becomes easier to make an accurate guess as to where problems will come and how they can best be resolved. The first attempt at the task is always best conducted using the battery of systematic techniques and checks suggested in this section.


## Parents

A school's obligation to its children's parents is at two levels. Dealing with individual parents, their needs, enquiries and problems, is one; and working to provide opportunities and events for them to encounter the school as a group on parents' evenings or in a school-based association, is the other. At both levels, Deputies are closely involved and take major responsibility, for instance in dealing with parents who have complaints, or in acting as liasion person for a parents' association.

Through direct practical contact, Deputies both play their leading role as representatives of the school and have the experience which enables them to judge the school's basic policies for parental communication and involvement. A typical transaction involves being the first member of staff to deal with a visiting complaining parent and having to make enquiries about the fact of the complaint, which may concern unsuitable placing in a subject option, something a teacher is alleged to have said to the child, or just lost property. Longer, usually calmer appointments are arranged for parents to discuss a child's problems at home or at school and to decide jointly upon a course of action. In both cases, the Deputy should involve other staff, in giving advice, possibly in person, or to act as consultant in providing information about a particular child's learning needs or behaviour in the classroom.

The first type of encounter tests the ability of the Deputy to act as a role model of skilful dealing with parents on a professional and social level, usually in the presence of other staff. The second involves assumptions about teaching and learning, the ability of the professional to diagnose specific learning needs, and the willingness of individual teachers to question their own classroom practices at times when disruptive behaviour in the classroom is under discussion. Both require a regular experience of the way teaching staff and parents understand and interpret school policy.

Dealing with an individual parent can place the Deputy in a particularly exposed position. An unsatisfied individual can always complain further, to the Head (who may use the Deputy to deal with particular parents, or types of enquiry if at all possible), or beyond. Here, the local authority, or even local politicians and the press, are involved if circumstances are extreme or a sense of proportion is lacking. Within the school, the Deputy's effectiveness in this field is also assessed by other staff. Deputies are judged to be effective here when they can:

1 Explain school policy clearly and convincingly at the parents' own level in language which is understandable to them. They should neither be patronising, nor attempt to mystify people with professional jargon.
2 Defend, or if necessary apologise for, the actions of a teacher, while still commanding the confidence of the teacher and parent involved.
3 Be able to counsel parents and tactfully insist upon parental responsibilities as well as rights, where appropriate.

A clear set of objectives in advising parents or dealing with their complaints forms a basis for understanding between staff and parents. It helps to build the partnership between school, parent and pupil. If this aspect of relationships is successful, then there is a better environment for events and activities such as parent-teacher associations.

Parental choice of school has, since the 1970s, placed schools in a position of having to compete for pupils (or at least to maintain an image which is successfully attracting parents to choose it). For some schools this has been a threat, for others it has created a stronger parental bond with the institution, and commitment to its continuing strength through active involvement in school activities. At once, two issues present themselves which directly affect the responsibility of the Deputy Head and define some commonly delegated tasks:

1 Questions of boundaries between professional and lay persons are raised in cases where a minority of parents have strong opinions about the school's policy over such matters as streaming, school uniform or subject choice.
2 The management of the school's public image cannot simply be left to chance, but must be the subject of deliberate control, and involve the mobilisation of support from parents and within the community.

Where questions of lay-professional boundaries occur, the Deputy recognises them as such by carefully explaining the school's objectives and the need for them to be developed with the interests of all pupils in mind. At parents' evenings it is important to distinguish between comments which really represent anxiety over the case of an individual pupil, and those which constitute a groundswell of opinion. In the latter case, the Deputy has to assess what has been heard from several parents, and the feelings of staff who may also be in touch with the particular parent or parents involved, such as the head of year, or the form tutor. They provide corroboration that a general mood among parents has reached the stage at which the Head will have to reconsider policy either in meetings of the Head and Deputies, through workings groups within the school, or through a parent-teacher working group.

Schools' public images are affected in many ways by uncontrollable factors. Word of mouth information affects the thinking of parents of pupils at feeder schools. This in turn could be linked to other considerations, such as drab buildings in a poor state of repair, the previous status of the school prior to comprehensive reorganisation, or rumours about the strength of discipline in the classroom (or lack of it). A school in a socially disadvantaged area will find it difficult to attract pupils from more privileged areas, unless it can offer a speciality or unusual attraction in its curricular or extra-curricular activities.

At the same time, a Deputy can be responsible for initiatives which build upon the school's strengths, serving to advertise them to the wider community as well as to raise the morale within the school. A Deputy with responsibility for public relations should adopt a planned policy including the following:

1 Notifying local radio and press of all special events and achievements.
2 Ensuring that the school's publications, including publications of pupil's own work, are distributed widely in the local community to parents and to feeder schools.
3 Preparing material to welcome new pupils and parents to the school, which may take the form of a prospectus, or a video presentation.

4 Maintaining high standards of pupil appearance and behaviour outside the school.

5 Ensuring that pupils' achievements and group efforts are in evidence at public events. A band, a model-making society or a drama group, as well as a sports team, may make appearances at summer events and exhibitions at the weekend as well as in the feeder schools during the winter.

6 Arranging events for intending pupils and parents which ideally allow them to visit the school during the day while it is in action.

7 Securing the co-operation of local industry, through parents, governors and friends of the school, to make available special opportunities for pupils, including travel, equipment and advice on particular aspects of the curriculum related to expertise available in the community.

These aspects of management may involve a large number of other interested staff. The greater the interest and willingness to help, the more important it is that efforts are co-ordinated. Events should be spread across the calendar, publicised to maximum effect, and, at the planning stage, talked through by the member of staff responsible with the Deputy who has oversight of this vital part of school life.

# Industrial relations

The changing form of industrial action in schools has involved Deputies more as they have had to administer schools against a background of unpredictability and daily change created by the effects of industrial action. They have had to make difficult personal decisions about the form of support that they can give to their own trade-union colleagues at the same time as carrying out management functions. This tests the attitude of the Head both to the action and to expectations placed upon the role of the Deputy at such times.

A trend in industrial disputes has been to move from making centralised employer-union negotiations the primary scene of conflict, to the enforcement of various work-to-rule actions based upon an evolving legal interpretation of the minimum requirements of the teachers' contract and conditions of service. When the minutiae of daily transactions in the school are administered by a Deputy Head, including the classes to be taught – or covered in the absence of a colleague – and the number of pupils in a group, then there is a potential for the creation or resolution of conflict, depending upon the way in which local union representatives interpret their function in the light of national union policy.

While the Head is faced with the pressure of accountability to governors and local authority, as well as sharing the complaints from parents which come in to the school if pupils are sent home, the Deputy is generally faced with securing the smooth running of the school and assessing the administrative consequences of a given form of action such as a half-day strike by a selected group of teachers. In such cases, the Deputy must be seen neither to be enhancing the effects of lawful industrial action nor to be subverting it by underhand methods.

Lambert (1982) suggests that during industrial action, the emphasis should be upon the free flow of information between unions and the Head and Deputies and that 'Meetings at school level should concentrate on finding common or complementary interests arising at other levels, i.e, on 'integrative' rather than 'disruptive' bargaining (p. 141). This involves 'role distancing' when working in the process of negotiation, so that inter-party bargaining against a background of mutually acceptable, previously established, ground rules takes place. The alternative – that of personalising issues – is to be avoided, whether by Head and Deputies or by union representatives. Aggression or intense feelings become institutionalised in the accepted procedures, so that, as far as possible, the normal business of the school and working relationships can continue.

The Deputy is in a position of having to log and produce constantly updated information at times when industrial action is at its height. This includes being able to produce details of staff required to cover absent colleagues as well as to assess instantly which classes will be affected by half or whole-day strikes, and when letters must be taken home by pupils to warn them of impending action. Staff 'cover totals' are best registered on computer programmes which can provide weekly or daily printouts of information if necessary. As strike action involves selected teachers rather than the whole union membership for a particular school, it is necessary to warn pupils' parents in advance that they will be at home. This is difficult when pupils are taught in different option groups, and the assembling of lists of pupils affected may be virtually impossible unless incorporated on a computer database in an accessible form. If the alternative is to spend hours compiling and collecting lists and updating them without clerical assistance, then priorities must be established as to whether or not this is the best use of a Deputy's time.

In part, industrial action over conditions of service can take the form of putting pressure on the Head and Deputies, regardless of which union they themselves are in. The checking and rechecking of information can disrupt all other normal forms of work, and it is essential that the burden of such action is borne equitably by the Deputies or at least rotated from time to time if the action continues for some time. This may be considered a legitimate form of action if the intention is to bring the normal working of the school to a halt until better conditions can be established, but, like all forms of action relying upon local enforcement at school level, there is a danger of it being applied differently from school to school. In circumstances like this it is important to know how the action is being applied in other schools within the same authority, and whether the problems encountered are shared or unique to the one institution. In the case of the latter, it may be possible for the Head, acting on a Deputy's information, to undertake further negotiations with the school union representative.

The most difficult decision for a Deputy to make is when conscience dictates that colleagues should be supported in the industrial action they are taking, but the Head does not agree. (In many cases, the Head may support the action, and hence there is no conflict.) The clash of loyalty here can only be resolved by considering the merits of the case, the background against which action is being taken, and its likely consequences. Another equally contradictory position to be in is when the ethos of a particular union membership in a school, or attitude of a particular union representative, attempts to distance Deputies from colleagues by emphasising their position as 'management' and, by implication, supportive of the powers ranged against the teachers' claims or campaign. This approach may be intended to undermine the Deputy's position as a colleague. It disrupts the tradition of management of teachers by colleagues, inherent in the widely accepted model of Head and Deputies as 'leading professionals'. The only response to such tactics is for Deputy Heads to act as individuals with political consciences. They should never accept a superficial interpretation of their position which either automatically brands them reactionaries opposed to any form of industrial action by staff, or, at another extreme, leads to their attempting to seek cheap popularity by joining in any form of industrial action regardless of its justification.

Industrial action comes in phases, according to the mood of teachers across the country and the reactions of groups of staff in individual schools. Whatever its form or timing, it has implications for the dynamics of interaction within the schools. Groups of staff more or less in favour of action will form themselves, occasional inter-union rivalries or tensions are manifested, and comments by the Head and Deputies may be analysed at a time of heightened perception in order to discern where loyalties lie. At this time, one of the most valuable contributions the Deputy can make is to distinguish and confirm the fact that there is life after a long dispute, and that the school will return to a normal or even better state of affairs when it is over.

# Buildings

In an age when larger schools have Bursars or Administrative Officers, one Deputy Head is, nevertheless, often still responsible for overseeing the state of buildings and the way in which pupils are using and caring for them, as well as for ensuring that they comply with Health and Safety at Work legislation. It may also be necessary to 'chase up' repairs and maintenance. If this is not obviously the work of the educationalist, then ensuring that the buildings are hospitable and welcoming to parents is.

A Deputy with responsibility for the state of school buildings will find it useful to obtain a briefing from the relevant department of the local authority, as well as to build up a list of telephone numbers for contact in emergency. These will range from the entry under 'Gas' for leaks, to the number of the local authority building services department. Also to hand should be records of repairs undertaken recently, repairs in hand and non-urgent repairs which have been deferred. If such a system does not exist or has been allowed to fall into disuse, it is vital to re-establish record-keeping procedures. The inevitability that some repairs will be required as a matter of urgency for health and safety reasons means that copies of requests, reminders and dates and times of telephone calls to follow up reports should all be logged to show that the Deputy responsible has taken all reasonable steps to follow procedures in operation.

The request system for repairs should allow for some responsibility to be shared by subject leaders for their particular areas. A 'request for repair' form, with a tear-off slip to confirm that it has been received or action taken, is useful here, but this system should be backed up by regular tours of inspection, if necessary in the company of the Head. An example of a 'request for repairs' form and registration system is given in Appendix 7.

Going beyond the overseeing of the procedural aspects of buildings management, and the chore of having to make sure that relevant departments do not 'pass the buck', oversight of buildings offers the Deputy the opportunity for managing the image presented by reception and foyer areas. Deciding which part of the building is most often seen by visitors and parents can be helpful in choosing a suitable area for a regularly changed display of pupils 'work and photographs of out-of-school activities such as school trips. There should be a reception area in which visitors can wait to be seen for appointments, and this should be near to office staff or those with responsibility for the reception of visitors. The area should be checked daily by the Deputy responsible for buildings.

Organisation of the care of the site, additional to that of caretaking staff, may be undertaken by teams of pupils with responsibility for different parts of the school, internally and externally. To ensure this, a Deputy should co-ordinate the allocation of form tutor rooms, and the year, house or other pastoral groups which occupy the buildings during registration or break times. One way to encourage care is to encourage pupils through pastoral heads to take a pride in their part of the building, to make it their own with displays, or classroom-wall newspapers, and to have a system whereby particular groups of pupils have 'territory' in the form of suites of classrooms into which other pupils may only come by invitation.

Maintenance of good, informal relationships with the caretaker and cleaning staff is also important in receiving early warning of problems in particular areas. Signs of graffiti or ill-use of a particular room will often be spotted first by cleaners (who have their own strong opinions about rooms, their state, and which rooms or groups of rooms are best or least-well kept). Information gleaned tactfully from them may help in identifying which staff or groups of pupils are having problems and where assistance might be needed. If the opportunity is taken to compliment cleaning staff on a job well done, or on special efforts made after clearing up in exceptional circumstances – after leaking pipes etc – then the co-operation and goodwill gained can provide unexpected bonuses later. This is reinforced on occasions when legitimate complaints are made. If they are listened to by a Deputy Head, cleaning staff can feel that their opinions are taken notice of by someone in the senior management group. Action taken should also be stressed where appropriate.

Oversight of buildings is, essentially, the undertaking of delegated authority. It can be stressful where responsibility is being taken without the power to get things done, especially if industrial action or underfunding makes reasonable maintenance impossible. However, provided the necessary administrative arrangements, as laid down by the local authority, are observed with efficiency, the task does allow the Deputy to take considerable initiative in promoting the buildings for the sake of the school's image, as well as to make sure that the work of an important element of the non-teaching staff is given its due esteem.

# Primary school liaison

A large secondary school in an urban area may receive pupils from numerous contributory primary schools, although it is likely that most pupils will come from a few major 'feeder' schools. In a rural area of scattered population with smaller primary schools, the number tends to be larger. Distance and time create obstacles to be overcome in communication between schools, but when a single Deputy is responsible for the managing liaison, it is possible to spread responsibility by making sections of middle management contribute to the process.

Subject heads should be aware of:

1 The main approaches and schemes of work used in teaching English, Mathematics and Science by the primary schools.
2 Differences in teaching style and expectation placed on pupils, particularly the extent to which the final year of primary school has been structured to provide some induction into the generally subject-based timetable of the secondary school.
3 The need to avoid duplication of subject content.

Pastoral heads need:

1 To have access to transfer cards or relevant documents.
2 Awareness of special needs of pupils with specific remedial requirements in literacy and numeracy skills, as well as early warning of acute behavioural problems or emotional needs. These should be treated in confidence.

Although the Head may wish to develop relationships with the primary school Heads, the co-ordination of the actual transfer of records, the placing of pupils into tutor groups, the management and storage of written records and a programme for reception of new pupils before the end of the summer term are all tasks for the Deputy. The assistance of a Head of First Year or Head of Lower School would be expected in a larger establishment.

Where transfer of records is concerned, it is important to be aware of how much information is likely to be contained on these. Some schools prefer to place as little as possible on record, especially with their 'problem' pupils, in the hope that they will start with a 'clean sheet'. However, some standardised test data is essential in order to screen out pupils with special educational needs. If it is not easily available, then it must be gathered. The administration of standardised tests of literacy and numeracy skills is best carried out by teachers with the pupils before leaving primary school. Attempts at testing in the first weeks in a new school usually produce misleadingly poor results.

For information to be gathered effectively, the responsible members, either of the English and Mathematics departments or of the Remedial and Assessment Section, should report directly to the Deputy on their programme of testing and findings as they emerge. Their visits to the schools should be co-ordinated to avoid duplication. Later, informal relationships built up between staff involved at the two schools can assist in the wider process of ensuring curriculum continuity.

Another important part of primary-secondary liaison is to provide opportunities for both parents and pupils to visit the school and to feel confidence in it. In the year preceding entry to the secondary school, there is a case for all Deputies and a number of other senior staff being available to show interested parents round the school at a number of times during the week.

The arrangement of a series of events over the year, including drama and music groups visiting primary schools, helps to build up confidence and may assist 'wavering' parents to make up their minds about choosing the particular secondary school which is doing so much to make their child feel welcome. A day in which intending pupils visit the secondary school with their own teachers and have the opportunity to meet their new house or year head and form tutor may be more helpful than the traditional evening event for parents, although this may also have to be held for information purposes. Such a day should contain a minimum of information sessions, allowing just enough to enable the new pupil to know what is essential, and then be followed by informal activities based around discussions in small groups. Serving refreshments adds to the sense of occasion. For this approach to be successful, the purpose of the day must be made clear to the primary school involved, and the organisation of the programme in school should be co-ordinated, preferably by the Deputy responsible working with a team of teachers who are due to be involved with the following year's intake group.

The next stage is to make a careful plan of the first day in school for newcomers. It may start before or slightly later than the day for the rest of the school in order that any preliminary snags or omissions with lists can be sorted out and pupils be placed securely in their tutor group rooms for registration. Now is another time to be reminded of school procedures and who to go to for help should it be needed. This is eased when a member of staff always shares responsibility for induction with the relevant Deputy, and where induction is viewed as a year-long process, forming part of an active tutorial or social-education programme.

Finally, the interest of the primary schools in how their ex-pupils are progressing should not be forgotten, and liaison should allow for them to have the opportunity to see and hear about outstanding pieces of work, as well as about subsequent achievements of pupils in gaining training opportunities and places in higher education. Only a Deputy Head is usually in a position to make sure that the many aspects of primary school liaison are carried out in full by the variety of staff involved.

## Responding to local authority advisers and Her Majesty's Inspectorate

Members of both these bodies work with Heads and report on schools, among other responsibilities. They may engage in dialogue and inspecting activities which involve the Deputy Head in two roles, either as an extension of the Head's areas of responsibility, or as individuals performing tasks in their own right. The local authority advisers, or inspectors, as they are called in some locations, share (with Deputy Heads) a lack of legally defined powers, and a considerable variation in their actual influence from place to place and individual to individual. Sturt (1985) describes the job of local education authority advisers as 'the eyes and ears of the Chief Education Officer' (p. 164), but goes on to emphasise their helpfulness in providing information of a sort Deputies find valuable:

> They are certainly not just concerned with gathering intelligence for the CEO, though this is an important part of their function, and from them you can find out what people are thinking at County Hall, how the authority is likely to respond to a certain application or scheme, or what sort of priority is likely to be accorded to this or that plan. (p. 165)

Another writer, observing the work of one team, suggested that advisers had a particular influence upon the Deputy. Small (1984) found:

> A highly experienced team who had worked together for many years, who knew the local scene well, and built up networks and contacts, and indeed had been on interviewing panels for large numbers of those currently working in the authority. This means that one or more advisers are likely to have had a hand in the Deputy's own appointment, and to see themselves as guiding and counselling the individual through a career as a Deputy, and inevitably undertaking a degree of formal or informal appraisal of performance. (p. 318)

A state of affairs such as this creates a potentially ambivalent relationship, because the same adviser has to relate to other middle management staff within the school, to the Head, and to other advisers. Good advisers see their role as being to work for the benefit of the authority as a whole. Those with a rigid subject-based perspective, having never had experience themselves of working at a level apart from that of head of a subject department, are likely to be more limited. It falls to the Deputy Head involved in timetabling or staffing adjustments to make difficult decisions about the distribution of resources, to compromise over rooming requirements, or to decide whether a teacher can or cannot attend a course, given the availability of staff to cover the absence. A good adviser is discreet when discussing the practicalities of school administration with staff, and will take account of the problems a Deputy faces here.

While work on appointments and redeployment is likely to be conducted directly with the Head, based upon logistical information provided by the Deputy, advisers may also be in a position to work directly with the Deputy in providing school-based in-service courses. Other approaches include monitoring probationers, helping to induct new staff, curriculum development initiatives (which may be teacher-centre based) and team visits to particular schools or departments.

In all cases it is necessary for the Deputy to understand the pressure of workload faced by advisers, especially at times of rapid staffing change or when other pressures such as financial reductions are in evidence. On the other hand, it is usually the thankless task of the Deputy as much as the Head to make advisers aware of the resource implications of some of their proposals, and to keep suggestions for innovations or new syllabuses within the bounds of what can be offered in the school over a particular year. Advisers working for smaller authorities are in a position to spend proportionally more time in each school, to have conferences at which most of their specialist subject heads will attend and to achieve a degree of coherence in the approach to their subject which is more difficult to accomplish in larger, more physically widespread authorities. This must affect the degree of input they are able to make into particular schools. It should also allow for an expectation of responsibility to and communication with the Deputy to be maintained.

Her Majesty's Inspectorate has formal responsibilities to the Secretary of State to report on the efficiency of the educational system. The best and most succinct account of its functions and organisation is found in official literature (DES, 1985). Purposes and methods of inspection are described in the Inspectorate's own publications (HMI, 1983 and HMI, 1986). One independent view

of Her Majesty's Inspectors comes from a highly experienced Head
(Sturt, *op.cit.*):

> They are civil servants, but on a rather special footing. They are
> appointed officially by the monarch in council, though in fact on the
> recommendation of a selection board including the senior chief inspector
> and other senior civil servants. There is some argument about the actual
> degree of independence that they enjoy. They are proud of it even
> if reluctant to exercise it in case it may be shown to be illusory. In
> one important respect they enjoy a special privilege in that their
> responses have a protected status and may not be altered without
> their agreement, even by the Secretary of State. They are, nevertheless,
> subject at least to the subliminal pressure of educational fashion. I have
> been dealing with them for rather more than twenty years and while
> I have indeed noted with pleasure one or two charmingly gifted eccentrics
> who have swum against the tide, I would say that the Inspectorate
> has seemed to me generally to have reflected the prevailing trend in
> politico-educational thought. (p. 163)

This gives an idea of the uncertainties of HMI's status and
something of what to expect when dealing with them. The frequency
of involvement with HMI may be limited to the occasional visit
to a particular department, or solely to the Head, especially when
a new appointment has just been taken up. However, considerable
demands are made on Deputy Heads at times of general inspections
of schools to provide detailed information about staffing, staff
deployment, curriculum and pastoral arrangements. A general
inspection can have the effect of forcing a disorganised school
to take stock of its systems for making information available, and
to become aware of empirical evidence of such matters as teaching
loads, gender bias between options, the degree to which pupils
are attracted to the school from within its normal catchment area
or beyond, and variations in performance expressed in examination
results between departments, and within the same department over
a number of years.

To teachers poorly versed in curriculum debate, and those who
tend to take a parochial, limited view of the requirements placed
upon them as professionals, a visit from HMI may be an upsetting
experience as they find themselves being judged by criteria of which
they were previously unaware. If this happens, then it indicates
a failure by the Deputies to have maintained a climate of debate
and information within the teams of subject or pastoral leaders
(although it is also possible for the failure to be unavoidable in
schools where a Head with esoteric or narrow views has effectively
stifled discussion of ideas which would otherwise filter into the
school from outside).

Good Deputies are informed about HMI thinking both by reports in the professional press, as well as through reading samples of HMI reports on individual schools. However, the range of demands made for information prior to a general inspection provides a working model of good practice for the monitoring and storing of data for which Deputy Heads should be responsible. Apart from staffing deployment and curriculum analysis, which have been dealt with in the section of this chapter on timetabling, the Deputy's own library of working documents of syllabuses, schemes of work, pastoral arrangements, analysis of examination results and entry procedures, option choices, six-form policy, homework procedures, records of rewards and punishments, and details of accommodation – its size, specialist facilities and location – should be retrievable without long hours of work.

Individual HMIs inspecting a school are guided by inspection schedules and their own training (which is not generally open to outsiders, although much of the thinking and 'flavour' of their approach can be inferred from reading their publications). They may be seen as complementing and extending the guidance available from local authority advisers. Like the local authority advisers, their subject-based structure imposes certain limitations, although moves towards looking more specifically at management processes, and other practices such as Community Education which do not fit into rigid subject boundaries, mean that a greater dialogue with Deputy Heads as well as the Head is likely to be necessary at times of inspections.

## Students, probationers and new staff in school

One person should take overall responsibility for the induction of new staff into a school. While the care of students, probationers and others places specific demands on subject and pastoral heads, there are cross-school needs which have to be catered for. A Deputy is in the best position to oversee these and to be the member of the senior staff to whom each newcomer can relate. Another variation of this common arrangement is for one Deputy to be primarily responsible for the programme followed by new staff, but that at times of high staff turnover or teaching practice numbers, the Deputies and the Head each take responsibility for one or more individuals. In a large school, a professional tutor responsible to the Deputy may also assist.

When receiving students on teaching practice, it is necessary to be clear about the aims of the training institution and its course structure. Time should be made to visit the institutions which require places for teaching practice in order to understand their expectations and to become involved in dialogue about the problems which students are encountering in school. It also allows for a good working relationship to be built up with a person who can be contacted in case of difficulty. For this reason, a Deputy with a whole-school view is best placed to deal with problems at an individual level where, unless the case is serious, it is not felt necessary to involve the Head. The Deputy is able to monitor the flow of information and requests from departmental and pastoral heads as well as to look after students at given points in the year, for instance at the start of teaching practice and towards the point of final assessment.

With probationers, the school's responsibilities are greater, although some of the processes of induction may be similar. There are a larger number of requirements to give support. Informal needs include:

1 Sorting out domestic arrangements and a place to live.
2 Understanding the ethos, pace, and implicit values of the school, including the specifics of behavioural expectations placed upon pupils in the classroom.
3 Understanding staffroom relationships and expectations.

Other needs are more easily stated on paper and in formal sessions. They may range across the following:

1 Understanding the school's policies about teaching and learning, including preparation and marking of work, homework policy and assessment procedures.
2 Knowing about pastoral structures and the system of referrals for pupils.
3 Having appropriate syllabuses and schemes of work to hand.
4 Having trouble-free access to teaching resources within the department, as well as audiovisual equipment and library stock held centrally.
5 Being able to resolve problems of ordering stock, finding keys to rooms, knowing when and if petty cash may be used, all as quickly as possible.
6 Procedures for registration, lateness and absence of pupils.
7 Procedures for staff requests for leave of absence and absence due to illness.

Much formal and informal briefing will automatically take place through the subject and pastoral heads responsible, but their stated responsibilities outlined on job descriptions should be reviewed from time to time under the heading 'Responsibility for new staff'. The Deputy is in the best position to make practical recommendations here, having directly co-ordinated their efforts.

From the individual member of staff's point of view, it is easier to contact a head of department or other future colleague with questions about syllabuses or where to look for a flat, than to bother the Deputy Head, but the Deputy should ensure through day-to-day contact that such communication is taking place. No future colleague should suffer from unnecessary anxiety or apprehension when this could be dispelled by personal contact and provision of adequate information. In a large department, it may also be advantageous to ask a colleague to act as mentor and guide for the first term of a newcomer's appointment. This relieves the load upon the departmental head and provides a readily approachable source of help, as well as spreading opportunities to other staff to develop an interest in staff development. Such an arrangement should always be agreed with the Deputy so that nothing is taken for granted or overlooked.

The form of appraisal used, and proformas to be completed for interim and final written reports on students and probationers, should be shown to the individual and discussed at an early stage. This allows each aspect of the appraisal to be talked about and interpreted in a way which is meaningful to the person involved. For example, 'Preparation of material' may mean mere booking out of resources from a department's stock cupboard to a relatively passive probationer, who may not understand the importance and credit attached to layout, readability, variety and differentation of interest level to the assembly of materials for a second-year mixed-ability English class. The Deputy will know sufficient of each department's work to suggest that a positive approach to the departmental head is made for guidance in such cases.

A school-based tutorial programme can provide opportunities for induction of all new staff with special 'annexe' sessions for probationers, if they form a group, or planned one-to-one sessions if there is only one probationer on the staff. It should serve the purpose of conveying essential information about the school as well as allowing for new staff to meet and discuss common experiences. An example of an induction tutorial programme is given in Appendix 6. It is advantageous for some sessions to take place in the absence of the Deputy responsible, possibly under the guidance of an informal and approachable pastoral head. Sharing and experiencing problems is an important part of interchange between new and inexperienced staff, and this is sometimes easier to do away from the person with a formal responsibility for appraisal.

As the year unfolds, the Deputy should check that needs are being met when they occur: classes settle down, for better or worse, and there may be a need for advice about handling particular groups which was not obvious at the beginning of the year. After several months' service in the school, there should be an opportunity to observe other staff at work in subject areas apart from the one in which the individual is mainly based. This should supplement as many chances as possible to see others at work within the same subject area. It is also valuable for probationers to visit other schools, such as the local primary schools which contribute pupils, and to go into other educational institutions such as the local College of Further Education, or different types of schools in a neighbouring authority.

A Deputy with responsibility for new staff is essentially taking over a part of the Head's delegated powers which cannot be effectively dealt with by the Head alone in a large school. The Head may, nevertheless, wish to have social contact with new staff, and to welcome them to the school, as well as to oversee the process of appraisal. The Deputy, though, should be in a position to see that all necessary administration is done, and reports returned in connection with the requirements for probationers and students, as well as to develop and perform the demanding skills of counselling and tutoring an important section of the school's teaching staff.

# 7 Conclusions: Deputy Heads and schools

A central argument of this book has been that Deputy Headship is more than mere preparation for Headship and that Deputies fulfil both shared and specific functions with senior management teams. The excellence of such teams is essential for the Head and staff to be properly supported, and therefore for the successful running of the school. We have seen that the Deputy's contribution to the team is a complex affair: much more than a simple, cosy conformity is required of an individual in the 'leading minister' model of Chapter 5. There may even be times when a degree of healthy conflict has its place in challenging complacency and ensuring that decisions taken are the best rather than the most comfortable. With this degree of commitment, and the fact that some Deputies see their own future as Heads, there are bound to be instances where disagreement may be deep. An analogy could be made with military command here, when it is as well to remember Montgomery's (1958) observation:

> The point is that honest differences of opinion are almost inevitable among experienced commanders, especially if they are also men with very definite views of their own. (p. 352)

In school, the questions for the men and women concerned are: given the commitment, experience and ability to take decisions which are expected of a good Deputy, is there not an inevitable tension between the Head and Deputies? If not, and a different, less assertive role is considered more appropriate, then is there any way in which the ideal Deputy Head is ever likely to make the highest calibre of Head?

A means of harnessing the dynamics of individuals in a strong team is through a more carefully defined placing of the legal status of senior team members within the school's management and administration, and this is explored later in this chapter. There is always a balance to be struck between the need to achieve a rational discharge of management functions, and the desire to continue to maintain friendly working relations with fellow senior managers even when there is a disagreement of principle. In this atmosphere, it is possible to use the Deputy Headship years as a stage at which initial training is acquired for future Headship. It is desirable to structure opportunities to enrich the role of Deputy while simultaneously preparing its holders for the opportunity of promotion. This is best examined by comparing the experience of Deputies with their needs as Heads-to-be.

# The Head-in-waiting stage

Experience as a Deputy was not always a requirement for Headship in the secondary school: Weindling and Earley (*op.cit.*) detected a significant move towards appointing Heads almost exclusively from the ranks of Deputies, whereas formerly a small but significant proportion of Heads had not served in the Deputy position. Referring back to data from the early 1970s, they went on to suggest that as many as 52% of Heads were chosen from Deputies prior to comprehensive reorganisation, but that the move directly from departmental head to Headship had now become virtually impossible (p. 20). In a period of twenty years from 1965–85, service as a Deputy Head, among other things, became established as a preparation period for Headship. The same study found that:

> While all the experience gained as a class teacher, form tutor, head of department and head of year was seen to be beneficial, almost all the Heads said that the most valuable experience was obtained during their period as a Deputy Head. (*ibid.* p. 39)

Given that this was the case, a number of experiences were seen as valuable, according to the authors' recommendations, including:

1 The opportunity to chair meetings and working parties.
2 Involvement in job interviews and governors' meetings.
3 Managing innovation.
4 Contacting parental and community groups, HMI and LEA officers and advisers.
5 Opportunity for regular career discussions and the chance to improve qualifications where necessary through attending courses.
6 Job responsibilities should be rotated.
7 Deputies should spend more time standing in for the Head.

8 Visits, exchanges and secondment to industry and other schools are valuable. (p. 184–6)

Each one of these training opportunities should also be linked directly to the needs of the school at a given time. There is nothing more calculated to arouse cynicism among staff than a Deputy who is being sponsored by the Head to promote initiatives apparently with a view to establishing a future curriculum vitae, rather than working on initiatives which arise from a careful analysis of the institution in which a wide range of staff have been consulted and involved. This is especially the case when a large number of initiatives are being encouraged in schools either by government or the DES. The temptation is to undertake many projects superficially, without the support of staff, and not to follow through their implications when external encouragement fades or is withdrawn. An example of this was found in the numerous schools which set up 'Language Policy Across the Curriculum' working parties after the publication of 'A Language for Life' (Bullock, 1975). Deputies were often directed to chair in-school groups, lacking time or resources, with the glib intention of effecting major changes in the habits of teachers and their attitudes to learning, in a process which would have also required massive injections of time and finance to re-equip the schools with books and learning materials. Much good was done, and a gradual shift in attitudes effected with many of the staff involved, but the result of trying to do too much at a localised level, without co-ordination, was that teachers were less likely to respond to future exhortations to change without adequate support.

This means that Deputies should always consider the depth and lasting nature of innovations for which they take responsibility and, again, only undertake them as part of a process which is fully supported by the whole senior management team. The responsibility should be real rather than superficial, so that the Deputy gains something of the 'hot seat' experience which later forms one of the most problematic steps from Deputy Headship to Headship reported by Weindling and Earley (*op.cit.* p. 185).

Secondments both to industry and to other schools are a useful way of broadening experience and providing a background which can allow for injections of additional experience into the home-school setting. For Deputies, secondments should be carried out with particular foci in mind. A week shadowing an industrial manager enables observation of meetings, priority setting and personnel management to be made, as well as allowing exploration of the differences between the ethos of school and industrial management. Visits to other schools allow for specific systems, such as vertical age-grouping in tutor groups, to be observed, with the opportunity to report back on its effectiveness. They may also give opportunities for the Deputy to join another school's senior management team as an observer to experience another style of Headship at first hand, permitting the sort of judgements which will be helpful in future Headship. Such visits help to avoid the parochialism and isolation which more inward-looking teams may develop without knowing it.

## Beyond charisma

The *Ten Good Schools* (HMI, *op.cit.*) view of the Head's leadership function created a yardstick for success which bordered on the mystical, and took no account of the advantages to be gained from the strengths of a team approach to managing schools. The success or otherwise of all staff in the school, including the Deputies, was seen as being derived from the essential qualities of the Head. In practice, one or more good Deputies can do much to balance the weaknesses of a Head who underperforms in certain aspects of management, whether it be in maintaining the discipline of the school or in being aware of current demands for innovation in the curriculum. Without this realisation, there tends to be an implicit search for 'hero' figures who carry within themselves an undefinable charismatic quality. In itself, this is supposed to resolve quickly all the awkward and untidy issues which otherwise require a plodding, rational approach by a large number of people listening carefully to each other and working together to develop the school.

One problem of this 'Superman' view of Headship (apart from the fact that it is restricted to the male gender) is that the role model presented both to the Deputies and to other staff is undesirable to emulate. It allows for only *one* leader at a given time. One or more other individuals measuring their own contribution by the criterion of the assertion of ultimate individual willpower in a school is a recipe for conflict and poor teamwork. A Deputy attempting to gain individual glory in the pursuit of ambition could only achieve it at the expense of wasting opportunities to learn about and contribute to group activity in the school. The teamwork really needed to create good schools is built up as part of a common commitment to improving the school as an educational environment, and this is only achieved within an atmosphere of sincerity and trust.

Greater security will be given to Deputy Heads to perform their task as their position becomes more formally recognised and accepted, not just within the school, but beyond. Their role is too little understood by local authority officers, and even by some local authority subject advisers. A step towards establishing the distinct status of Deputy Heads in law was taken by the passing of the Education Act (No 2) 1986. Section 39 directs that the articles of government make particular facilities for the appointment of Deputy Head teachers which may in all important respects follow the procedures applicable to the appointment of Heads. Previously, Deputies were, like heads of department, pastoral heads or any other post-holder (apart from the Head) all classified together as 'Assistant Teachers' so far as Education Acts were concerned. The legal obligation to perform varying functions was determined more by the implied contract prior to the imposition of conditions of service. As Imison (AMMA, 1984, pp. 41–6) pointed out, a contract is affected by what was in the advertisement for the post, what was said at interview, and agreements reached by whatever means to change duties undertaken (usually by mutual agreement with the Head). Here, the contract is underwritten, but is a contract nevertheless.

Imison goes on to suggest that the job descriptions for Deputies should not be 'fixed and immutable'. Apart from being professionally disadvantageous, a person in a managerial position responds to numerous exigencies which could not possibly all be written down. In other words, the closely defined contract is not what is sought so much as the right to share a degree of legal authority with the Head, as well as the obligation of responsibility and accountability to outside interests which go with it. If by this we are closer to establishing the expectations placed upon Deputy Heads by direct accountability to parents and governors for aspects of work such as providing and explaining details of staff deployment to operate a part of the curriculum, or making available a report on sites and buildings and the progress of liaison with the relevant department of the authority, then the status of the post in the eyes of governors and others will be better confirmed. This might involve the need for larger schools to have other aspects of their management structures recognised and referred to in the articles of government, always provided that this did not create inflexibility for restructuring in response to alterations such as changing demands upon the curriculum, or variations in the size of a school's roll. It would also define particular consultative arrangements, such as a standing curriculum committee, to be chaired by a Head or Deputy, whose purpose should be the final forum in which proposed change could be discussed. Such structures could also make the Deputies formally responsible for sharing part of the Head's duties, including gathering information for the Head to present to

governors, as required under section 32(1) of the 1986 (No 2)
Act, where the governors may require reports from the Head.

The formal recognition of the importance of Deputy Headship
and of the growth of its responsibilities will require that proper
arrangements are made for clerical and administrative assistance,
and that more trivial tasks are more strictly monitored. An
anonymous writer (1980) in the *Times Educational Supplement*
experienced Deputy Headship as being:

> . . . at everybody's beck and call from the moment he or she first
> enters in the morning – not the building, but the car park: from the
> Head, the caretaker, and his cleaning ladies to the most junior teacher
> and the youngest pupil.

Worse than this, the same writer complained, as do many abused
Deputies, that much of the work undertaken could be done by
administrative assistants for the examples given, including:

> Examination arrangements.
> Deciding which blackboards and windows need replacement.
> Key-cutting.
> Ordering gas cylinders for mobile heaters.
> Distributing syllabuses.

While the organisation of administration for some tasks has been
dealt with in earlier chapters, the examples given here are not
untypical and do illustrate the need to avoid the tendency in some
schools to make the Deputy the most highly paid junior clerical
assistant in the education service!

While it is true that the occasional copying out of a list of names
assists in gaining familiarity with them, constant copying of lists
is best undertaken by computer. With this in mind, the ILEA
committee (1984) recommendations for *Improving Secondary
Schools* included a much greater use of word processors and other
computer-assisted administration to relieve both Head and
Deputies from 'multitudinous clerical duties' (pp. 114–5). Bulletins,
circulars, statistical information and timetable information can all
be stored efficiently on computer. Copying out a timetable by hand
in the form of staffing master, year timetable, room timetable or
subject timetable, is time wasted. There is no virtue in spending
hours on this task when the information could be typed once into
a machine which can then print out the common data in each
of its permutations instantly.

Similarly, the writing of reports, filling in of official returns to
request repairs, and correspondence with other schools could all
be undertaken by a Deputy supported by a typist. This raises
the question in large schools as to whether or not Deputies should

have their own secretaries, who, like the Head's secretary, fulfil a personal assistant role. It is a matter for judgement whether such a service helps the Deputy to cope with routine duties more effectively and give more attention to staff, as well as finding more time for thought and discussion with fellow members of the senior management team, or tends to act as an unnecessary obstruction to direct contact with the majority of staff. This symbolic presence of a secretary and all that that means in the form of status must be considered carefully for its effect upon communication, as against the advantages it would bring. Certainly, given the finance available to most schools, such an arrangement would not generally have high priority, and staff reaction to such an allocation of resources would have to be taken into account. The best compromise is to make a realistic assessment of the administrative support needed by the Deputies as a group over the school year, including 'peaks' such as the point at which options are negotiated or individual staff timetables are to be published, and for this to be available from one or more members of the clerical staff whose own office should be based in close physical proximity to where the Deputies work.

# Future influences

Changes in the nature of schools will lead to changes in the nature of Deputy Headship. At the most basic level, new tasks will be undertaken. Granting schools more financial autonomy means a greater involvement in finance management and accounting, for instance. At another level, the management procedures which are derived from a particular school's basic commitment to beliefs such as equal opportunities will make further demands upon a Deputy Head's ability to relate the aims of policy to middle management processes, and capacity to communicate well with classroom teachers.

Although Deputy Headship will continue to embody numerous local variations and oddities, future change is likely to be brought about as a result of three main factors:

1 Decisions to redefine and change the function of Deputy Head, connected to the restructuring of management procedures within individual schools. This will be most apparent in schools which have undertaken reviews or self-examination of their fundamental aims, in response to pressure from staff, the Head or elements within the community.

2 External influences and challenges to the organisation and nature of teaching and learning from centralised directives arising from

government or HMI initiatives, as well as the changing consensus – both public and professional – about the social and political purposes of the schooling system.
3 Changing expectations and requirements – legal or otherwise – of the role of the Head.

To anyone outside the school system, the publicity surrounding the launch of official papers and pronouncements would suggest that external influences place the largest single demand upon schools. Their cumulative result is unknown, because the effect of a proposal only becomes clear when it has been negotiated at the level of an individual school, and often at the level of an individual classroom. An example of this is the quality of experience of pupils with special needs who have been integrated into 'mainstream' schools from special schools. Only the personal commitment of staff allied to a development of new professional expertise could make a success of such a change in policy by central direction.

Many of the new influences on schools, at first sight, would suggest an increase in standardisation. The imposition of testing at set stages in the pupil's career, of national curriculum guidelines and of teaching contracts could all be taken to imply a future in which Heads as well as Deputies will have less room for initiative. Their job, it might appear, would be to pass on and administer central directives. If this is the case, then the system will falter under the weight of its own unforseen contradictions. Deputy Heads who are left constantly struggling with interpretations of a rule book tend to develop ways of coping better with that rule book, rather than putting it aside to concentrate upon essential issues of relationships within the school and how they affect the quality of teaching and learning in the classroom.

Instead, it is more probable that schools will continue to remain highly individual, requiring responsive leadership which releases the talent and creativity of people, rather than line management. A school is more than a neutral, value-free administrative entity, and the more external influence which is brought to bear upon it, the more differences manifest themselves. Each instithtion distinguishes itself by its responses to the nature of its catchment area, that area's traditions of reaction to formal schooling, beliefs about education, and availability of employment prospects. These give standardised curriculum or organisational packages contrasting receptions in different institutions. Another influential factor lies in the personality of strong Heads and the emphasis they may place, for instance on traditional forms of discipline, on equal opportunities, or on the arts; all lead to varying 'flavours' to school life. A particularly strong influence on individual differences between schools is staffroom culture, whether it is a reaction to some of the factors outlined above, or arises from movements within the staff itself. One distinctive staffroom culture may contain a strong element of commitment to anti-racism and anti-sexism. Another, perhaps in a different geographic setting, is dominated by ex-grammar school staff with an apparent desire to see most educational issues from the point of view of the local squirearchy. Both types of staffroom culture would be strongly resistant to crude and simplistic attempts to interfere with professional autonomy in any way.

Above all, the atmosphere of individual schools and the influence of staffroom culture have strong influences upon what pupils actually learn. Again, this is regardless of planned curriculum outcomes and the results of formal testing. Coercive management can do little to interfere with the autonomy of the teacher in the classroom: pupils are very sensitive to asides, to the teacher's tone of voice, or to insensitivity and platitudes. Bad timetabling, poor physical conditions in school, insensitive, standardised curriculum objectives, and poor relationships between staff will be felt and noticed by young people even when teachers try to remain professionally discreet about such problems.

All this has implications for Deputy Headship and its place within school management of the future. The more we examine the changing and contradictory demands made upon the school by society, and take stock of the rapid demands for curriculum and examination reform, the more necessary it is to be aware of the neglected influence of the workings of internal power relationships on which the Deputy Head has a key regulatory role. This means that a traditional way of discussing schools as 'Head and staff' is no longer adequate when considering how shared beliefs and values articulate themselves. The complexity of the process is illustrated by Hoyle's (1986) comments on authority and influence within the school:

> The distinctive configuration of power relationships in the school is shaped by the interpenetration of the authority and influence of the Head and the influence of teachers. The Head enjoys a high degree of authority but there are constraints on its exercise which lead to a greater reliance on a wide range of both sources and bases of influence. These restraints on the Head's authority include: the loosely coupled structure of the school, expectations about the appropriateness of the exercise of authority in culturally and morally orientated organisations, and the countervailing resources of influence enjoyed by a professional staff. (pp. 75–6)

Management literature on Headship which seeks to subsume such a range of human endeavour under the one concept of 'leadership' is in danger of obscuring more than it illuminates. The quotation above implies the need for a system of group or team management in which 'culturally and morally orientated' issues are dominant in matters of daily administration. To do otherwise is to put Heads in the dangerous position of oscillating between heroine/hero and scapegoat figure, ignoring the contribution of a strong supporting team which the Deputies should provide.

This book has shown the individual Deputy Head as being in a position to confirm and evolve the values and meanings of an institution through force of personality, as well as through the practical administrative decisions which are taken each day. These daily actions and procedures have the authority of senior management, and the resources associated with it. The Deputies extend Headship, giving it vitality by contributing ideas to the Head, and sharing the Head's views and opinions as a result of negotiation and the quality of discussion. At this level it can only be generated in a small team of influential, individual, leading professionals, whose efforts give shape and direction to wider participation by staff in policy-making. When this process is working properly in the team it becomes a stimulus and model for similar activity within other groups of staff across the school. The very success of the group approach relieves the institution of the apparent tyranny of unbridled egotism implied in older celebrations of the role of the Head.

Sharing in the creation of a school's beliefs and meanings involves the Head and fellow Deputies in enabling the participation and commitment of the staff as a whole. The reality of school life here is generated by deeper processes than superficial daily procedures, as Hoyle (*ibid*) points out:

> In matters of organisation and leadership schools are unlike many other kinds of organisations. All organisations display epistemological, cognitive and logical limits to the operation of rationality, and schools are no exception. Moreover, schools are organisations in which symbols, as manifest in language, actions and artefacts, are particularly potent at many levels, not least the managerial level. Thus management is much concerned with the symbolic construction of meaning especially in the relative absence of formal and explicit procedures. Meaning has to be construed from a complexity of signs, and can easily be misconstrued. (pp. 170–1)

At this level, the Deputies are as necessary as the Head in maintaining an awareness of what staff, parents and pupils are really thinking. However external forces seek to impose change upon schools from without, the business of ensuring an integration of professional views and approaches within an institution will continue. This in itself can only be achieved by discussion and debate between professional peers, rather than by the setting of disembodied objectives by legislation. Such discussion goes on in corridors, at break and in the Head's and Deputy Head's offices as well as in the formal setting of a staff meeting or working party. The more a management group is working with and as part of a staff, rather than at a hierarchical distance, the more likely it is that the reforms required of changing schools will be successful. Those externally imposed political reforms which ignore such a partnership will be likely, of themselves, to fail by not recognising this.

Two possibly contradictory movements are to be found in schools at present. The first is a tendency to standardise institutions through the imposition of teacher contracts and a national curriculum. The second is a tendency to require some form of local accountability with an increased power of parents to choose between schools and to have better access to information about them. Both take place against a longer term development of more professional management skills among Heads and Deputies in which the dilemmas and problems of running large schools are gradually being faced and resolved successfully. Not the least of these issues centres on the changing nature of Headship. A proper account of the changes in the power and authority of Heads, as well as of the new challenges they face which would have been undreamt of by their historic predecessors, is quite incomplete without an awareness of the role played by the Deputy or team of Deputies.

This means that, far from Heads responding to initiatives on their own, proposals reaching the school will first be discussed by a highly professional team of Head and Deputies prior to consideration by other groups within the staff. Deputies' views will be of particular importance because, as we have seen, they take a primary responsibility for seeing that the daily running of the school is actually taking place. They must process and decide upon priorities for the implementation of any initiative, whether it is passed down by central government or arises from the efforts of parents and the community.

Working with a professional staff within the school, there are clear limits to the usefulness of coercive power as a means to achieve results. A school which relies upon contractual obligations will always be a long way from being a professional community of teachers. Deputies, even more than Heads, will have to maintain their position as leading educators. This is necessary to be able to move autonomously within the internal political system of the school – winning support for plans and initiatives as well as maintaining cohesion among staff. As education changes, Deputy Headship offers one of the most satisfying positions available to anyone in the school. Deputies have the opportunity to ensure that formal policy is made into classroom reality, and that decisions are not arrived at without knowledge of the real experience of young people in the school. They are able to share the experience of children – their growth, doings and reactions – by teaching alongside their colleagues at the same time as helping to control the institutional opportunities for good teaching. Deputy Headship offers a unique chance of being part of a school staff, knowing teachers' feelings and aspirations well, and being able to make positive use of this knowledge in leadership.

At the same time, it offers an especially privileged relationship with the Head, by virtue of position, which allows an exceptional opportunity to influence and shape the practice of Headship itself. Good Deputies enhance, encourage and facilitate the working of good Heads – the sort of Heads who naturally operate an open, accessible style of management involving staff across the school as well as the community beyond. They have the opportunities to be creative, to initiate policy themselves, and to start projects which have a particular chance of success through the awareness of and access to resources – human and financial – which the Deputy's day-to-day working knowledge makes available. This deep knowledge of people and resources can be used to maintain and build up areas of experience and consultancy to help practical teaching work, without the constraints of some of the commonly found boundaries of subject or pastoral divisions and other school hierarchies.

Deputies are also especially privileged by occupying the sole position which allows effective training and preparation for Headship, if they desire to make that their next personal career objective. Their experience of senior management may also equip them for further stages of a career in advisory work, lecturing or administration; although the increasing satisfactions of the post make it a very desirable end in itself. The post's satisfactions are derived additionally from the fact that while each Deputy is unique in the school and holds particular responsibilities, it is also held alongside one or more other Deputies of parallel status, holding complementary responsibilities. In this way it allows for vigorous and rewarding participation in the business of senior management, but without the potential loneliness or isolation which can so often be felt by Heads.

Finally, Deputy Headship is a post which is at last coming into maturity in its scope and expectations. Nationally, and in individual schools, Deputy Headship has gained its just recognition. Schools with a team of Deputies who possess commitment, expertise, experience – and not a little inspiration – are bound to be places which are well-run, cohesive, and personally enriching for staff and pupils alike. This in itself describes what most people would call a good school. The building of that achievement with others is the greatest fulfilment of Deputy Headship.

# Appendix 1

## 'Broad' and 'specific' job descriptions for Deputy Heads

### a. Broad job description for Deputy (pastoral):

- Deputise in the Head's absence.
- Co-ordinate pastoral heads.
- Co-ordinate pupils' reports and profiles.

### b. Broad job description for Deputy (curriculum):

- Co-ordinate subject heads.
- Create the timetable.
- Staff development.

A request for further details of a post producing the above should be answered with other documentation about the school in general. The manner in which these jobs are expected to be performed would then become more clear.

### c. Specific job description for Deputy (pastoral)

- Contribute to policy in management team meetings.
- Lead team of pastoral heads.
- Organise induction, profiling, social education programmes.
- Organise active tutorial programmes.
- Oversee extra-curricular activities.
- Assist in interviewing and staff selection.
- Oversee 'statementing' of pupils with special needs.
- Deal with acute disciplinary crises.
- Determine composition of tutor groups.
- School assemblies.
- Admission arrangements for new pupils.
- Edit parents' newsletter.
- Liaison with primary schools.
- Oversight of careers guidance programme.
- Prepare timetable for completion of reports.
- Organise parents' evenings.

### d. *Specific job description for Deputy (curriculum):*

- Deputise in the Head's absence.
- Contribute to policy in management team meetings.
- Lead team of subject heads.
- Oversee teaching programmes.
- Develop classroom ethos and learning policies.
- Oversee development of and store copies of schemes of work and syllabuses.
- Record staff deployment and staffing needs.
- Create the timetable.
- Staff development and INSET
- Assist in interviewing and staff selection.
- Oversee screening and diagnostic assessment programme.
- Deal with acute disciplinary crises.
- Determine and oversee procedures for grouping pupils in groups for subject learning, i.e, 'setted', 'streamed' or mixed-ability and mixed-age groups, as applicable.
- School assemblies.
- Allocation of new pupils' personal timetables during the year.
- Daily cover for staff absence.
- Oversee all new curriculum development projects.
- Oversee staff professional library.

### e. *Specific job description for Deputy (administration):*

- Contribute to policy in management team meetings.
- Oversight of buildings, repair and maintenance.
- Staff records.
- Complete returns such as DES form 7.
- Year 3 option choice programme.
- Liaise with parent-teacher association.
- Public relations officer.
- School assemblies.
- Deal with acute disciplinary crises.
- Assemble agendas and take minutes of meetings.
- Examinations secretary.
- Health and Safety at Work records and meetings.
- Pupils' bussing arrangments.
- Capitation and finance records.
- Library, resources and audiovisual aids.
- Arrangements for school trips and exchanges.

The specific job descriptions shown above would be expanded or contracted according to the interests of the individual in post. In larger schools, a considerable amount of delegation and secretarial help would be expected for the range of responsibilities to be discharged effectively.

# Appendix 2

## A year's curriculum decision-making chart

### Term 1

- Cover last-minute vacancies or engage supply teachers.
- Arrange option programmes for any newly admitted fourth or fifth years.
- Make staff deployment analysis.
- Complete curriculum analysis.
- Head and Deputies to start curriculum review.
- Set up working groups as required.
- Summarise and consider effects of:
  a. New legislation.
  b. HMI or subject association reports.
- Review findings of screening and diagnostic assessment on intake year.
- Review examination results from previous summer.
- Review changes in curriculum recommended by report-back of working groups.
- Pencil in provisional 'blocking' for the next timetable and discuss at least with Head and Deputies.
- Advertise and fill vacancies for next term.

### Term 2

- Analyse results of internal practice examinations.
- Finalise intended syllabus changes for next academic year.
- Start options guidance programme with year 3 (sometimes leading on from foundation work on choice and careers in the previous term).
- Update and print pupil options workbooks.
- Update and print options information handbook for use of pupils and parents.
- Commence options choice programme, with analysis of initial choices and note trends.
- Interview individual pupils about their option choice.
- Introduction to the sixth form programme with fifth years.
- Provisional sixth-form subject choice and pupil counselling.
- Establish provisional assumptions for staff deployment.
- Draw up provisional timetable structure.

– Examine anticipated vacancies due to retirement, etc, for end of summer term.
– Advertise and fill vacancies for next term.

## Term 3

– Departmental reviews of achievements and goals for curriculum and staff development over the next year.
– Update staff deployment analysis and establish known or anticipated vacancies. Advertise and fill vacancies for next term.
– Consider redeployment, losses or increases in staffing and its effect upon the curriculum.
– Consult or inform subject heads about likely teaching teams within timetable blocking, and likely second and third subject teaching by particular members of staff.
– Publish timetable blocking, consult subject heads, and resolve problems through agreement or otherwise by a stated date.
– Timetable scheduling or 'staffing up'.
– Publication of timetable.

# Appendix 3

## Questions to explore aspects of Deputy Headship in selection interviews

### a. Opening questions:

- Tell us about your career to date.
- Tell us about your present school. What kind of school is it?
- What are your impressions of this school? How does it compare with your present school?
- What are the areas of responsibility which attract you most?

### b. Exploring previous track record and extent of present technical knowledge:

- Can you give an example of a change in management you have brought about within your present post?
- What is your approach to timetabling?
- How do you establish curriculum continuity between primary and secondary schools?
- How do you expect your job to change in the context of: changing rolls/new forms of assessment/government policy etc?
- What is the relevance of . . . (a particular official report, recent legislation or other major publication of the last five years)?
- How do you unite academic and pastoral work more effectively?
- Specific questions on themes especially relevant to the particular school and its priorities, for example: urban education, rural schooling, the 11–13 age group, multi-cultural education.
- How do you organise a core curriculum for the lower school?
- How much paperwork is necessary to the work of the Deputy Head?
- Could you name one thing that you would like to see improved in your present school?
- How do you monitor standards?
- How have you prepared yourself for this post?

### c. Questions to investigate interpersonal skills:

- How do you ensure that staff maintain good standards?
- What is the importance of loyalty for a Deputy Head?
- How do you get on with other teachers at your school?

- What makes a good leader, and how do you get people to do what you want them to?
- If a young teacher comes to you for help with a particularly difficult class, what guidance do you give them?
- A pupil or parent makes a justified criticism of a colleague. What do you do?
- What do you do about a member of staff whose performance is unsatisfactory in the classroom?

### d. Personal qualities and philosophy of education:

- What do you enjoy most in teaching?
- What are your main characteristics as a person?
- What sort of work do you do best?
- What do you perform least satisfactorily?
- What sort of sense of humour do you have?
- What do you expect school to provide for your own children?
- Is there one Deputy Head you particularly admire in your present school, and what is it that makes you do so?
- A good Deputy stretches her/himself and others in the process. What does this mean to you?
- How do you manage crises?

### e. Concluding questions:

- Would you be prepared to identify one main weakness you have?
- What, above all, attracts you to this particular school?
- How do you see your career developing over the next five years?
- Are there any questions you would like to ask us?

# Appendix 4

## Basic timetable data

1. Figure 4.1 illustrates the first year of an eight-form entry school in which the timetable for each half year is identical. In the diagram the subscript number indicates the number of periods (within the twenty-period week) for which each subject is taught.

See Figure 4.2 for other conventions based upon Eustace and Wilcox's system.

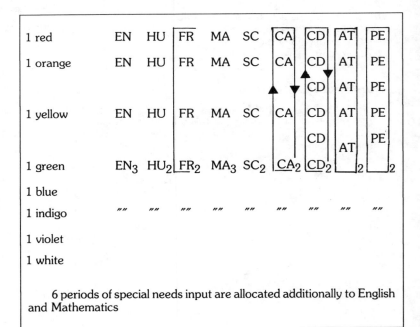

**Figure 4.1:** curriculum analysis in diagramatic form.

(This system was developed in DES COSMOS courses, and refined by Eustace and Wilcox (1977). Many local authorities have their own variations.)

AT
AT
AT
AT
AT₂

The four tutor groups are 'supported'
by an additional member of staff for
Active Tutorial Work.

CD
CD
CD
CD
CD
CD₂

The four tutor groups are divided into
sets (but ability is not the criterion
of division). The sets follow a rota
system. In this case 'CD', an abbreviation
of CDT, includes a rota of CDT (including
Art and Design, as well as Home Economics).

PE
PE
PE
PE
PE₂

For PE, groups are setted, but not by
ability.

FR
FR
FR
FR₂

French is setted by ability at an early
stage.

**Figure 4.2.**

2. Figure 4.3: may also be used to analyse the deployment of staff to their first teaching subject, and to review the distribution of responsibilities by gender and age.

| Name | Age | Allowance | Qualification | 1st Subject | 2nd Subject | Number of yrs. in post | Number of yrs. to retirement | Responsibility (Tick if actively seeking other posts outside) | Gender | Other qualifications |
|---|---|---|---|---|---|---|---|---|---|---|
| G. Adams | 33 | D | BSc/PGCE | Maths | — | 4 | — | Head of Maths | F | |
| J. Bowen | 56 | B | Cert. Ed. | History | English | 19 | 4 | Humanities Stock control | M | PSV licence |
| C. Brown | 40 | B | B.Ed. | English | P.E. | 12 | — | Assistant Head of English | F | |
| D. Cox | 22 | Main Grade | BA/GCE | French | Spanish | Probationer | — | | M | |
| J. Cronshaw | 31 | B | MA/PGCE | English | Drama | 5 | — | Oral English | M | LRAM (piano) |
| S. Datta | 35 | Deputy Head | B.Ed./MA | Physics | Maths | 4 | — | Deputy Head (Curriculum) | F | First Aid Cert. ASA Teachers Certificate. |

**Figure 4.3:** Lists of teaching staff with responsibility held.

| Room | Specialist | 1st | 2nd | 3rd | 4th | Unoccupied |
|------|-----------|-----|-----|-----|-----|------------|
| W1 | Lab | 16 | 1 | — | — | 3 |
| W2 | Lab | 18 | — | — | — | 2 |
| S1 | Geog | 12 | 6(Maths) | 2(Eng) | — | — |
| S2 | Geog | 18 | — | — | — | 2 |
| S3 | English | 16 | 2(ATW) | 1(French) | — | 1 |
| S4 | English | 18 | — | — | — | 2 |
| Etc. | | | | | | |

**Figure 4.4**: room usage analysis (based on a twenty period week).

3. The same information can be expressed as percentages of time occupied by the designated 1st subject, and others. See figure 4.4. If suites of rooms have been designated, it is also valuable to analyse the percentage of time for which each subject is successfully placed in its designated rooms for each period of the week.

# Appendix 5

## Standing agenda for routine weekly meeting of Head and Deputies

Most of these items will be taken quickly or omitted in order that one or two major items of business can be treated in depth.

1 Review of diaries: routine appointments and time out of school for the following week.
2 Events and school-based meetings for the following week.
3 Items for staff weekly bulletin.
4 Staffing: intention of staff to seek posts, references taken up, expected future staffing needs as a result of movement, staff morale.
5 Buildings and site: health and safety at work matters.
6 Pupil welfare, discipline, morale, movement, punctuality, etc.
7 Special problems regarding the start or end of term.
8 Reports from meetings of subjects heads, pastoral heads or working groups.
9 Reports from departments.
10 Timetabling developments.
11 Screening and diagnostic testing reports.
12 Primary school liaison reports.
13 Finance and capitation.
14 Correspondence and circulars.
15 Local authority initiatives.
16 Professional press and research reports.
17 Other major discussion items to be raised by the Head or Deputies for further discussion at a separately convened meeting.

Each member of the group should be in possession of the standing agenda in order to prepare themselves to contribute to the meeting, and to attend with the necessary information or documents to brief colleagues as necessary.

# Appendix 6

## Induction programme for new staff and probationers

### Term 1
(Pre-term school visits should precede this).

*Meeting 1*
- Welcome from the Head.
- Discussion of school procedures based around staff handbook.
- Introduce school professional tutor, if applicable.

*Meeting 2 (probationers only)*
- Introduction to expectations of the year, including an outline of the appraisal features in operation.

*Meeting 3 (probationers only) External function*
- Local authority reception for probationers at teacher's centre.

*Meeting 4 External function*
- Reception and recruiting meeting for trade unions.

*Meeting 5*
- Review of the first term's progress, discussion of shared problems and solutions.

### Term 2

*Meeting 1*
- The school and its community session with Deputy Head (community) or Deputy with oversight of multi-cultural education.

*Meeting 2*
- The school's curriculum.
- Classroom styles and practical teaching skills.
- Preparation for visits to other institutions and departments.

*Meeting 3*
– Audiovisual aids and reprographics: developing expertise.

*Meeting 4 (mainly probationers but others welcome)*
– Report back on visits to other departments and institutions.
– Session on the role of the form tutor.

**Term 3**

*Meeting 1 (probationers only)*
– Pastoral case studies, discussion with a pastoral head (without the presence of a Deputy to allow frank interchange about potential problems).

*Meeting 2 (probationers only)*
– Managing personal time.
– Dealing with fatigue or stress and relaxing.
– Discussion (this is best chaired by the professional tutor or other experienced member of staff in the absence of the Deputy. A person with training in counselling might be particularly helpful here).

*Meeting 3*
– Comments and feedback on the year.
– Suggestions for improving the programme or changing input for the following year.

## School-based meeting for students on teaching practice

– Welcome from the Head.
– Discussion of school procedures based around staff handbook.
– Introduce member of staff with responsibility for students, if applicable.
– Audiovisual aids and reprographic facilities accessible centrally.
– The role of the Head of Department in assessing students' teaching practice performance.
– The nature and content of the appraisal form which the school returns to the student's own institution.

# Appendix 7

## Example of 'request for repairs' form:

| | |
|---|---|
| Department | |
| Date of request | |
| Room or location | |

The following repairs are requested:

Cause of need for repair (if known):

| For office use only | | | | | |
|---|---|---|---|---|---|
| Date received | Received by | Repair Order no. | Forward to LEA | Job No by LEA | Completed |
| | | | | | |

Other action taken:—

Reasonable date expected to be completed:

Signed _____

# Example of a repairs analysis file proforma:

| Date | Reported by | Room | Nature of repair or hazard | To whom reported | Caretaker LEA | If LEA date priority | LEA Job No | Ref. No. | Completion Date | Remarks |
|------|-------------|------|----------------------------|------------------|---------------|----------------------|------------|----------|-----------------|---------|
|      |             |      |                            |                  |               |                      |            | 1        |                 |         |
|      |             |      |                            |                  |               |                      |            | 2        |                 |         |
|      |             |      |                            |                  |               |                      |            | 3        |                 |         |
|      |             |      |                            |                  |               |                      |            | 4        |                 |         |
|      |             |      |                            |                  |               |                      |            | 5        |                 |         |
|      |             |      |                            |                  |               |                      |            | 6        |                 |         |
|      |             |      |                            |                  |               |                      |            | 7        |                 |         |
|      |             |      |                            |                  |               |                      |            | 8        |                 |         |
|      |             |      |                            |                  |               |                      |            | 9        |                 |         |
|      |             |      |                            |                  |               |                      |            | 10       |                 |         |
|      |             |      |                            |                  |               |                      |            | 11       |                 |         |
|      |             |      |                            |                  |               |                      |            | 12       |                 |         |
|      |             |      |                            |                  |               |                      |            | 13       |                 |         |

# References

AMMA (1984), 'Teachers as Managers : Deputy Heads and their Role', *Report of Conference for Deputy Heads,* Assistant Masters' and Mistresses' Association.

Anonymous(1986), 'The Grass is Greener ?' Times Education Supplement, 1.8.86.

Baron, G (1956), 'Some Aspects of the Headmaster Tradition' in *Leeds Research and Studies* (Vol 13); reprinted in Musgrave, P W (ed) (1970), *Sociology History and Education,* Methuen.

Belbin, R M (1981), *Management Teams : Why they Succeed or Fail,* Heinemann.

Benyon, G (1984) *see* AMMA (1984) above.

Bullock, A (1975) 'A Language for Life' in *Report of the Committee of Inquiry appointed by the Secretary of State for Education and Science* under the Chairman of Sir Alan Bullock FBA, Her Majesty's Stationery Office.

Burnham, P S (1968), 'Deputy Head' in Allen, B (ed), *Headship in the 1970's,* Basil Blackwell.

Bush, T (1981), 'Key Roles in School Management' in *Management and the School,* E323 Block 4 Part 3, The Open University Press.

Bush, T (1986), *Theories of Educational Management,* Harper & Row.

Coulson, A (1976), 'Leadership Functions in Primary Schools' in *Educational Management and Adminstrarion* (5)1, pp. 37–48.

DES (1985), *The Educational System of England and Wales,* Department of Education and Science.

Drucker, P F (1970), *The Effective Executive,* Pan.

Dunham, J (1984), *Stress in Teaching,* Croom Helm.

Eustace, P J, and Wilcox, B (1977), *Curriculum Notation,* City of Sheffield Education Department.

Forster, E M (1960), *The Longest Journey,* Penguin Edition (originally published by Edward Arnold, 1907).

Gilmour, I (1971), *The Body Politic,* Hutchinson.

Griffith, J A G (1966), *Central Departments and Local Authorities,* George Allen & Unwin.

Hamblin, D (1981), 'Pastoral Care and Pupil Performance', in Hamblin, D (ed), *Problems and Practice of Pastoral Care,* Basil Blackwell.

Hoyle, E (1986), *The Politics of School Management,* Hodder & Stoughton.

HMI (1977), *Ten Good Schools: A Secondary School Enquiry,* Her Majesty's Stationery Office.

HMI (1983), *HM Inspectors Today: Standards in Education,* Department of Education and Science.

HMI (Wales) (1984), 'Departmental Organisation in Secondary Schools' *HMI (Wales) Occasional Paper*, The Welsh Office/Y Swyddfa Gymreig.

HMI (1986), *Reporting Inspections: HMI Methods and Procedures*, Department of Education and Science.

Hunt, J (1981), *Managing People at Work*, Pan.

ILEA (1984), *Improving Secondary Schools: Report on the Curriculum and Organisation of Secondary Schools*, Inner London Education Authority.

Johnson, D, Ransom, E, Packwood, T, Bowden, K, Kogan, M (1980), *Secondary Schools and the Welfare Network*, George Allen & Unwin.

Johnson, K (1980), *Timetabling*,Hutchinson.

Lambert, K (1982), 'Micropolitics, Industrial Relations and the School in *Educational Management and Adminstration* 10(2) pp.139-43.

Lloyd, A (1986), 'The First 120 Days (Starting a Headship)' in *Human Relations in Education Series* (No 3), School of Education Publications, University of Nottingham.

Lyons, G Stenning, R (1986), *Managing Staff in Schools: A Handbook*, Hutchinson.

Marland, M, Hill, S (1981), *Department Management*, Heinemann Educational Books.

Maw, J (1977), 'Defining Roles in Senior and Middle Management in Secondary Schools' in Jennings, A (ed), *Management and Headship in the Secondary School*, Ward Lock Educational.

Montgomery, Bernard Law, Viscount (1958), *The Memoirs of Field Marshal The Viscount Montgomery of Alamein KG*, Collins.

Morgan, C, Hall, V, Mackay, H (1983), *The Selection of Secondary School Headteachers*, Open University Press.

Morgan, C, Hall, V, Mackay, H (1986), *Headteachers at Work*, Open University Press.

NAHT (1986), 'Appendix 6: The Role of the Head and Deputy Head in Today's Schools in *Proposals for a New Salary Structure for the Teaching Profession*, National Association of Head Teachers. (Unpublished draft report).

NAHT (1987), 'Deputy Head Teachers' Working Party of the NAHT in *The Role of the Deputy Head*, National Association of Head Teachers.

Open University (1981), *Management and the School: Course E 323*, The Open University Press.

Paisey, A, Spackman, B (1982), 'Secondary School Management: Deputy Heads' Perspectives of their Jobs in *British Journal of In-Service Education* 8(3), pp. 154-9.

Peters, R S (ed) (1976), *The Role of the Head*, Routledge & Kegan Paul.

Ribbins, P (1985), *The Management of Pastoral Care: Prescription and Practice*, Paper presented on 2nd November 1985 to a conference jointly organised by British Educational Management and Administration Society & National Association for Pastoral Care in Education at the University of Birmingham.

Richardson, E (1975), *Authority and Organization in the Secondary School*, Macmillan.

Slater, S M, Long, R S (1984), 'Whole School Evaluation and Staff Appraisal: A Practical Guide for Senior Staff', *The Journal of Evaluation in Education.*

Small, N (1984), 'Evaluating the Evaluators: the Role of the Local Education Authority Inspectors' in Goulding, S, Bell, J, Bush, T, Fox, A, Goodey, J (ed) (1970), *Case Studies in Educational Management*, Harper & Row.

Smetherham, D, Boyd Barrett, O (1981), 'Managing the Curriculum' in *Managing the Curriculum and Pastoral Care*, Course E 323 Block 5 Part 1, The Open University Press.

Spencer, A (1981), 'School Timetabling' in *Managing the Curriculum and Pastoral Care*, Course E 323 Block 5 Part 2, The Open University Press.

Stone, J (1986), 'The Role of the Deputy Head in the Secondary School' in *School Organisation* 16 (1), pp. 39–48.

Sturt, J (1985), *Managing the Secondary School*, Bell & Hyman.

Todd, R, Denison, W F (1980), 'The Changing Role of the Deputy Headteacher in English Secondary Schools' in Bush, T, Glatter, R, Goodey, J, Riches, C (ed) (1980), *Approaches to School Management*, Harper & Row.

Trethowan, D (1983), *Delegation*, Education for Industrial Society.

Weindling, D, Earley, P (1987), *Secondary Headship: The First Years*, National Foundation for Educational Research – Nelson.

Woods, P (1979), *The Divided School*, Routledge & Kegan Paul.

# Index